V for VICTORY

David Boyle has been writing about new ideas for more than a quarter of a century. He is co-director of the New Weather Institute, a fellow of the New Economics Foundation, has stood for Parliament and is a former independent reviewer for the Cabinet Office. He is the author of *Alan Turing, Scandal* and *Before Enigma,* as well as a range of other historical studies. He lives in the South Downs.

V for Victory

The wireless campaign that defeated the Nazis

David Boyle

THE REAL PRESS
www.therealpress.co.uk

Published in 2016 by the Real Press.
www.therealpress.co.uk © David Boyle

The moral right of David Boyle to be identified as the
author of this work has been asserted in accordance
with the Copyright, Designs and Patents Acts of 1988

ISBN (print) 978-0993523946
ISBN (epub) 978-0993523953

For Serena

Contents

"As an institution that could not tell a lie, they were unique in the contrivances of gods and men since the Oracle of Delphi. As office managers, they were no more than adequate, but now, as autumn approached, with the exiles crowded into their new sections, they were broadcasting in the strictest sense of the word, scattering human voices into the darkness of Europe, in the certainty that more than half must be lost, some for the rook, some for the crow, for the sake of a few that found their mark."

Penelope Fitzgerald on the wartime BBC, *Human Voices*, 1980.

"I imagined that I could see thousands of people, alone or in groups of two or three, huddled over muffled radio sets in blacked-out rooms in the homes of a country where I have never been, listening with me, to them. The V campaign was ... the voice in the darkness."

Joe Liebling, 'Colonel Britton and the Rhythm', *New Yorker*, Oct 1941

1

Introduction

"When the history of the war is written it seems likely that the V campaign will appear as something more than a propaganda stunt. It has certainly done much to make the people of occupied countries conscious of their national and international solidarity. Experience has shown that nothing can stop what Goebbels has called the 'intellectual invasion of the continent by the British radio'; an invasion of which the letter V was the symbol.
C. J. Rolo, American reporter, 1943

It was 6 June 1941, at fifteen minutes past midnight in continental time, three years to the day before D-Day, as it turned out. The British were preparing to march into Syria and Lebanon, the Germans were preparing to march into Finland and Russia. The war was entering a terrifying new momentum of its own. Those who tuned into the English language frequency of the BBC European Service that night, listening across a Europe occupied by the Nazis, heard for the first time an unfamiliar military voice, claiming to be a someone called 'Colonel Britton'.

Britton spoke with calm and reassuring authority. Not for long either, aware that his listeners may be listening in difficult circumstances and that listening to British broadcasts would probably be illegal, he spoke for just over four minutes, and – for the year in which he went on the air – never more than eight.

"Here in London, in the midst of this war, we still get messages and letters from across the Channel," he told the listeners, huddling round their wireless sets desperate to hear the programme *London Calling Europe.* "They come by all kinds of strange ways from France and Belgium, Holland and Denmark, and even from Poland and Czechoslovakia. There are so many of them that I've been asked once a week to reply to them. To us, these messages are inspiring. They show there's a remarkable toughness about the people of Europe – so tough that it'll take a lot more than these heavily armed but half frightened Nazis to kill."

Was this true? Was there a remarkable toughness about them? Neither Colonel Britton nor his colleagues knew, but they *hoped* there was. This was an experiment: that by asserting this toughness they would, in fact, call it into existence.

Actually, the man behind the voice was not military at all. It was Douglas Ritchie, a former *Daily Telegraph* journalist who was then Deputy European News Editor, nominally at the BBC, though actually control of European broadcasts had been made semi-independent from the BBC some months before. The V campaign which Colonel Britton was announcing was a joint project with his boss, Noel Newsome, and had been carried out in the teeth of opposition from the competing government agencies struggling for control of propaganda to Europe.

It was the beginning of an extraordinary freelance piece of broadcast propaganda, and it remains a potent memory today – a key element in the European Service's (and by default, the BBC's) formidable wartime reputation, credited with capturing the imagination of the occupied people's of Europe, revitalising their morale and fostering what eventually became the various resistance movements.

In real life, Ritchie was somewhat shy and self-effacing and held no military rank. Nor did he actually speak with the explicit permission, either of the War Office or the Ministry of Information. Nor was it an inspiring moment of the war. There had been a brief moment of elation earlier in 1941, when General Archibald Wavell succeeded in taking Tobruk, since then there had been reverse after reverse. And the dark continent, under Nazi rule across the English Channel, was silently ominous. Ritchie himself wrote later of the "terrible quiet" from there. In practice, it was unclear whether anyone was listening at all.

Those of us who know a little about the history of the Second World War, and who know what was to happen, are all too aware of the ferocious resistance movements that were to emerge to challenge the Nazis. But then, in the early months of 1941, they knew no such thing – and nor, except in a few pockets of occupied Europe, did the resistance movements yet exist. The V campaign, launched officially that night, was a first attempt to shape them – to give people the confidence to think independently again, to so blow on the embers of morale among the defeated nations of western Europe that they might one day resist.

So much of the background to the V campaign is now forgotten – the vitriolic war over the radio airwaves for the hearts and minds of Europe, the bitter battles over radio propaganda fought inside the British government, and the extraordinary success of the European Service, when 15 million ordinary Germans risked a death sentence every day to listen to broadcasts from London. But the aftermath of the V campaign lives on in the very mythology of modern Europe.

Colonel Britton broadcast every week for less than a year – a mysterious figure, the subject of much speculation on both sides of the Channel. But the paraphernalia of the campaign remains with us still in so many ways – the idea of simple acts of resistance, Churchill's ubiquitous V sign, but more than that too. There is an element of V that was, in some basic ways, part of the founding myth of postwar Europe. It provided hope that, one day, Europe would liberate itself – as indeed it did.

This is the story of the pre-eminent moment in the forgotten wireless war, when a few journalists – with no experience of policy or espionage, and practically without permission – launched one of the most effective press campaigns in history.

2
The Airwave War

"The BBC should have its place in future history books side by side with the fighting forces. The regular way it has carried on, even during the autumn months of 1940, while bombs could be heard falling in the distance, the almost unbelievably short time London was ever off the air, and the fact that the voices broadcasting never once changed their tone or faltered – all this is the admiration of everyone."
Letter received by the European Service from Italy, 1941

It was during the long, hot summer of 1943, that Friedrich Henning, a railway employee in Wurzburg, overheard two of his senior colleagues discussing the war. They agreed that the prospects were grim. Germany was fighting on two fronts and the Americans were going to provide the resources to invade.

Henning was a 34-year-old Nazi party member, frustrated and embarrassed to be working on the railways rather than being in military uniform.

Henning went to the local Nazi headquarters and denounced Max Heinrich and his friend Hans Vogel.

Research into denouncements of this sort suggests that Henning had some kind of continuing grudge against the man he was listening to, the railway inspector Heinrich, who was 47, but he never admitted this. He was advised to keep listening to what they said, noting down the times and dates of Heinrich's remarks, and to keep detailed notes about the conversations. For the next three months, Henning befriended Heinrich. He drew him and Vogel out in conversation and wrote down what transpired. It became clear very early on where Heinrich was getting his opinions from. He had been listening to radio broadcasts from London and had made some of the opinions that he had heard there his own.

By September, as the fighting continued on the eastern front, withdrawing before the assault of the Red Army, Henning had the evidence he needed – not just to prove defeatism but for the far more heinous crime of listening to foreign broadcasts. This was now becoming a serious case.

Back in August 1939, Hitler's deputy Rudolf Hess had suggested that listening to the foreign radio stations should be made illegal. Hitler's propaganda chief, Joseph Goebbels, was asked to look into the details. He drafted a brief law that Hitler signed immediately in the very first days of the Polish invasion. It was called 'Extraordinary radio measures'. "In modern warfare the opponent does not only use military means but also methods which influence national morale and are intended to undermine it. One of these methods is radio," it claimed. "Every word that the opponent broadcasts is of course a lie and intended to damage the German people."

There was intended to have an air of rhetorical gentility about it. Goebbels implied a paternal desire to save people's time, to avoid them suffering the rubbish that was being put out over the foreign airwaves. But at the heart of the proclamation was an edge of steel:

> "Anyone who intentionally disseminates information gleaned from foreign radio stations which is liable to threaten the defensive capability of the German nation will be punished with penal servitude, in particularly serious cases with death."

Listening to that peculiar world, swirling about

people's heads, with lies and truth doing daily battle with each other on both sides, was a dangerous business, as the railway inspectors in Wurzburg were to discover. In the middle of September 1943, Max Heinrich and Hans Vogel were arrested by the Gestapo on Henning's evidence. The local court sent them to the People's Court in Berlin. They were found guilty of listening to foreign wireless stations. Vogel was imprisoned and survived the war. Heinrich was sentenced to death.

A year after, on 26 September 1944, the day the Allied troops surrendered at Arnhem, Heinrich was hanged; they were the victim of what was, in effect, a wireless war. It had been five years since the war had broken out, and five years since the nascent BBC European Service had begun to evolve – and so controversially – into such a potent weapon of war.

It was 1 September 1939 when the European editor of the *Daily Telegraph*, Noel Newsome, was called in to see his proprietor Lord Camrose at 10pm and told he had to report the next day to Broadcasting House. The BBC's European editor had gone home with some kind of nervous breakdown. Two hours later came the news that German troops had crossed the Polish frontier.

Having arrived at a nervous BBC, Newsome asked to see the only person he knew there, a former *Telegraph* sub-editor, Douglas Ritchie. The two were to form a strong partnership together, and they would need each other's support.

Newsome himself was a good choice, a 33-year-old former boxing blue and a lifelong journalist. Both Newsome and Ritchie had worked abroad, Newsome on the *Malay Mail* and Ritchie on the *Rand Daily Mail* and *Johannesburg Sunday Times*. Both had gone to the *Daily Telegraph* in the run-up to war, with Newsome in charge of all the paper's coverage of the European crisis.

Having tracked down Ritchie, he dashed back to the *Telegraph* to organise a special edition of the paper, emerged at 7am and collapsed in a chair in a pub. He then arrived at the BBC, past the lines of children awaiting evacuation, to find he had a staff of only 30 to organise news bulletins in six languages (two years later it had grown to 500) and absolutely no instructions about what to do and how.

"From the start and right through the war, we were essentially back-room boys, anonymous and, quite appropriately, unhonoured and unsung," he wrote later. In the absence of any instructions, the first bulletins emphasised – quite inaccurately – Britain's determination to fight. Only the most bellicose statements were reported. The first instruction came only after the declaration of war, to broadcast a rather hopeless appeal to the German people to rebel against their leader.

In fact, the wireless contribution to the war effort was so nearly nipped in the bud. Prime Minister Neville Chamberlain had played with the idea of closing the BBC or taking it over completely at the outbreak of war. The early months were not auspicious either. "The BBC pours out into the air day by day an endless stream of trivialities and sillinesses," said the *Sunday Times,* "apparently labouring under the delusion that in any time of crisis the British public becomes just one colossal moron." Even the Labour leader Clement Attlee agreed that it was depressing. Millions of people listened in to propaganda German propaganda broadcasts, ostensibly as light relief.

It was a different news environment then. Naming merchant ships was strictly forbidden, and the location of air raids couldn't be published for thirty days. Then as now, there were strict rules about anything that could endanger military operations and, until 1940, the BBC was forced to read official press releases out in full. There were also regulations against publishing anything calculated to ferment opposition to the war – which at one stage came close to being used to shut down the *Daily Mirror*. As the Nazis swept across Europe, the government even bowed to pressure from the French, who had been keeping their own population completely in the dark, and censored news about where the Germans had reached.

Meanwhile, the Nazi's radio arm, Reichsrundfungesellschaft, kept up a constant patter of propaganda, news and comment, buttressed by the other radio stations as, one by one, they came under the control of the German military. It was heavy handed stuff:

> "The war criminal Churchill announced yesterday the systematic bombardment of the Italian capital. In the announcement, the brazen lie was presented to the world ... this is the kind of shameless duplicity with which Churchill prepares to get another devilish plan for his air force... The war criminal No. 1 attempts to shift the blame for this approaching crime by his shameless lying."

At one point during the war, Hitler's propaganda minister Josef Goebbels ruled that Churchill must never be named without the epithet 'whisky-drinking'. But this was the first wireless war; there were no rules to apply. Goebbels seemed at that stage to have demonstrated his mastery of the new communication technologies. It wasn't clear how to fight back.

Newsome and Ritchie felt differently. The output from Berlin in English seemed to them pompous and vainglorious, as the programmes were constantly interrupted by announcements from the Leader's Office of victories, followed by a war song. If it was considered important enough, the statement was read again, followed by the Hörst Wessel song and the national anthem. Then a warning: "A radio silence now follows." As early as 1941, one man was arrested for asking the bar staff at a Berlin restaurant to turn the broadcasts off.

German broadcasters seemed to be making patronising assumptions about their average listener. Newsome wrote later:

"He was not an adult like an English or American listener, chatting on equal terms with Roosevelt by the fireside, or hearing Churchill begin punctually, after a preliminary snuffle, a nine o'clock. He was not fit, and it might have been dangerous, to let him hear the experience of pilots and sailors who had not studied the directives of Reichskulturwart Hinkel of Truppenbetreuung."

This was a potential advantage to the new European Service, then based at the BBC, and Newsome sensed it early on.

As the Phoney War ended and the panzer divisions pushed westwards, Hitler's 'black' propaganda stations kept up a cacophony of voices emphasising the dangers to property and urging peace. The question was: how should Britain respond? There were deep divisions about propaganda, and not just which members of the cabinet would control it, though that was difficult enough. Behind the internal wrestling matches between ministers lay a very modern political issue, which has remained with the UK political scene ever since: a deep disagreement about Europe and Britain's relations with it.

Some, like Newsome, believed Britain had something to offer Europe, if they could speak clearly and honestly about why they were fighting. Others felt that any message had to be tailored carefully if any of the complex European nations were to follow it – especially a message as radical, idealistic and belligerent as the one that the BBC European Service was beginning to shape.

Critics inside and outside the BBC complained that this 'moral approach', the attempt to claim the moral high ground in the wireless war, also reflected Newsome's own personal agenda. He seemed to them an old-fashioned Whig, railing against Napoleonic tyranny. On the other hand, he contemptuously dismissed professional diplomats and propagandists as "too complicated" – he preferred what the historian Asa Briggs later called "the weapons of responsible journalism and ... the instruments of the clever advertiser" to put across British ideals and war aims. The trouble was, these war aims were disputed. Once Britain had survived invasion, the vacuum where they should have been became increasingly important.

All this was a dilemma for Newsome, Ritchie and their team. Yes, they should clearly concentrate on objective, factual, authentic news. Yes, the truth was a valuable lesson and would win them listeners – lying would not help them. But that wasn't quite the end of the argument. This was the beginning of the distinction between 'black' and 'white' propaganda. Black propaganda was based on blatant untruths. Neither the BBC nor their European Service would have anything to do with that. But what about 'white propaganda', the use of the truth to win the battle of ideas? It meant more than just objective news, but could broadcasters employed by the BBC do such a thing?

Criticising the BBC during the General Strike, Churchill had coined a phrase that 'you can't be impartial between the fireman and the fire'. The European Service was not so objective that they could contemplate the other side winning with equanimity – but could they do something to help the war effort? Could they, *should* they, actually campaign? Newspapers had a great tradition of campaigning, and Goebbels had shown only too well how radio could be adapted for war. The real question was how much the campaign to liberate Europe would compromise the truth of their bulletins. And would their superiors allow a campaign anyway?

For Newsome the real battle began in April 1940 with the disastrous attempt to prevent a Nazi invasion of Norway, when he and the rest of the BBC felt they had been tricked into broadcasting lies. Or as Churchill put it later: "Throwing dust into the eyes of the enemy".

Newsome's daily directives began to shape a daily line for the bulletins to take. There were parallel meetings in Berlin. Every morning at 11am from 6 September 1939, Goebbels would hold his own daily briefings. These were eventually attended by nearly 50 staff, most of whom kept quiet – those who did speak up usually regretted it.

Meanwhile, the black propaganda radio stations, set up by the Nazis, were also multiplying, including the new ones broadcasting to Britain and Radio Concordia, purporting to be by French communists, actually broadcasting from the basement of Soorstrasse 33 in Berlin.

William Joyce had read his first news bulletin on German radio three days after the start of the war, calling himself William Fröhlich (joyous). He was treated as a joke by the British press, who called him Lord Haw Haw because of his voice, but the authorities were terrified. They were scared of his trenchant criticisms of the British class system, and his appeal to the deepest fears of the British working classes, but most of all they were terrified of the listening figures. A third of the British population was tuning in to hear him every night in the early months of the war.

The message was also serious. Joyce may have been an obsessive anti-Semite, but he was no idiot, and he understood the importance of using English history – which he described as a struggle between Whigs ("grossly materialistic") and Tories ("mystical incompetents") – for his own ends. His message of social justice and his critique of City financiers was bound to have an appeal. The BBC desperately scheduled Gracie Fields to clash with him, in the hope that her appeal would draw listeners away, but it had little effect.

Much more effective than Lord Haw Haw was Paul Ferdonnet. He was the son of a teacher from Niort and became known as 'The Traitor of Stuttgart' for his promotion of the Nazi regime. He was one of the most skilful broadcasters of the war, operating out of Radio Stuttgart – one of a string of German-backed radio stations along the frontier with France, and broadcasting in French. He was lively and compelling and, in the uncertain months before May 1940, he built up a loyal following in France, and particularly among the troops. "Bonne nuit, les gars," he said every night. "Á bientôt."

"The English will fight to the last Frenchman," was his phrase. It was influential, powerful stuff. But what was most unnerving about him, and his menu of defeatism, was just how much he seemed to know. When four British officers had a row with a waiter in a Dieppe cafe, Radio Stuttgart described the incident nine hours later, including details of what they had to drink.

We will never know how much Ferdonnet contributed to the unexpected collapse of French morale. He was condemned to death in his absence by the French judiciary, but the damage had been done. On 13 June 1940, the French premier Paul Reynaud announced on the radio that they were surrendering Paris. The broadcast began with the Marseillaise.

"Whatever may come in the days before us, all Frenchmen, wherever they may be, must be prepared to suffer," said Reynaud. "Let them be worthy of our nation's past. Let them gather in brotherhood around their stricken fatherland. The day of resurrection will come." Listening in a radio shop in Limoges, Arthur Koestler described a large crowd around him listening in terrified silence. Some were in tears by end of the national anthem. At the final words, many others joined in.

"It was the first and last time that I have seen a crowd burst into tears on a political occasion," he wrote. At 11.30 that morning, the French army handed over Paris.

The occupation of France and the other European countries put the BBC's European broadcasts into a new perspective – but it was not quite clear what it meant. If anyone was going to encourage resistance to Nazi rule, it was probably going to be them, but there was a reluctance among the BBC mandarins to challenge the government when their charter was in danger of being revoked altogether. Newsome and Ritchie and those around them realised that, if they failed to provide reliable news, listeners would seek it elsewhere, and that meant they had to extract reliable information from the authorities.

This was the mistake Hitler was about to make in France. Part of the armistice signed in Compiègne was that French radio would shut down. This would have given a huge advantage to the BBC's new French Service and their news programme *Ici de la France*, if its presenter and production team had not decamped to Vichy. Radio Paris was relaunched a few days later by the new Nazi controllers of the city, led over the air by Friedrich Sieburg, a former social democrat and Paris correspondent of *Frankfurter Zeitung*. His programmes were brilliant, witty and above all useful. He broadcast long lists of people looking for work, and congratulated anyone providing work over the air.

Churchill sent a plane to Bordeaux to collect what he hoped would be an assortment of senior French officials, politicians and military men prepared to carry on the fight from London. When it touched down in Croydon, the only figure to emerge was the tall, arrogant one of the defence minister Charles de Gaulle. Less than a month before, he had led the only major tank counter-attack against the advancing Germans. His decision to board the plane had been an act of intuition rather than calculation.

On June 18, he was escorted into Broadcasting House by Newsome's assistant Leonard Miall and ushered into the studio where the French announcer was just reading the news. Surprised to see a French general, he stood up, bowed and banged his head on the microphone. Miall stood behind de Gaulle as he made his broadcast, rejecting the advice not to introduce himself as "Moi, General de Gaulle". No recording was made of de Gaulle's words but the phrase "France has lost the battle but she has not lost the war", which was used in millions of posters and leaflets in the months that followed, was not actually in the original broadcast.

It so happened that a titan of French theatre, Michel de Saint-Denis, had been among the

French forces taken off the beaches after being wounded at Dunkirk and he was asked by the BBC to front a new programme called *Les Français parlent aux Français* under the name Jacques Duchesne. This was an enormous success. The programme broadcast for the next four years, with a witty mix of humour, satire, comment and fun: it was hugely original and ahead of its time. Radio Paris replied with a programme called *Les Français parlent aux émigrés*.

"The émigré has always been wrong throughout history," said Pierre Laval, the dominant figure in Pétain's Vichy regime, but even he listened, fascinated, to *Les Français Parlent aux Français*.

It was harder to find native Germans to broadcast on the BBC German Service, for obvious reasons, and the decision was taken that the audience would be more likely to respond to foreigners. Even so, they needed to find people who really understood the way Germans thought, and one of those was Sefton Delmer.

Delmer was one of those peculiar personalities who find their niche in moments of chaos or conflict. He was the son of an Australian professor of English Literature, was born in Berlin and had been interned as an enemy alien as a child in the First World War. His knowledge of Germany meant that he had been in increasing demand as a journalist by the British press as Germany's future became an increasingly fraught issue. He had built himself an enviable reputation as a foreign correspondent before the war, covering Berlin for the *Daily Express*, during which he had befriended Goebbels. He had been the first British reporter to interview Hitler.

But all of this also made him a figure of some suspicion in British intelligence circles. He had struggled back to London through war-torn Poland after the outbreak of war and found himself under investigation by MI5 as a suspected enemy agent. Part of his problem was that he was too well-known to slip into an obscure job. Even the RAF was calling one of their barrage balloons over Dover 'Seftons' because people believed there was some resemblance with his rotund figure. It was a difficult period for him. He was desperate, in fact, to work for some branch of the intelligence agencies, knowing that his knowledge of the Nazi leaders was probably deeper than anyone else in the country.

His first break followed the appointment of Duff Cooper as Minister of Information in the summer of 1940. The style of Lord Haw Haw was obviously effective. Now that the BBC German

Service was running effectively, would Delmer do a weekly commentary in German? Of course he would, and over the next few weeks, the new commentators had worked out a rota for themselves. Dick Crossman, the future cabinet minister, who would soon have a key role in propaganda to Nazi Germany, would take Tuesday evenings; Delmer would take Fridays.

He arrived at Broadcasting House on the warm summer evening of 19 July 1940, to find the building camouflaged to avoid it being visible to German bombers during the Blitz. He was in some excitement, having prepared the bones of his first broadcast – but also aware that Hitler was giving a speech in the Reichstag that evening that he would have to reply to. At 6pm, the European Service staff gathered around the wireless to listen to it.

"It almost causes me pain," said Hitler from the platform, "to think that I should have been selected by Providence to deal the final blow to the edifice which these men had already set tottering… Mr Churchill ought for once to believe me, when I prophesy that a great empire will be destroyed which it was never my intention to destroy or even to harm… In this hour, I feel it my duty before my conscience to appeal once more to reason and common sense in Britain … I can see no reason why this war must go on."

Hitler sat down to tumultuous applause. Delmer's broadcast was due to go out in less than an hour. What they needed to do was to turn down the peace offer in such a way that their words could not be misunderstood. A simple no thank you wasn't really enough. Delmer drafted a reply that, after an initial pretence of deference to the German leader, built up to a crescendo of rudeness. "Herr Hitler, you have on occasion in the past consulted me as to the mood of the British public," he wrote. "So permit me to render your Excellency this little service once again tonight. Let me tell you what we here in Britain think of this appeal of yours to what you are pleased to call our reason and common sense. Herr Hitler and Reichkanzler, we hurl it right back at you, right in your evil smelling teeth."

Newsome read through the script and agreed. This was one of those occasions when it would only complicate matters to ask for permission. He had come to believe that, if he thought like Churchill did, then he would probably be doing the right thing. It was just after 7.30pm, an hour later in Berlin, when Delmer went ahead and rejected Hitler's peace offer without reference to higher authority.

In Berlin, the Rundfunk studios in Charlottenburg were crowded with officials and junior officers from the Nazi high command, listening to any clues from London about how the peace offer had been received. Standing at the back, CBS correspondent William Shirer saw their faces fall when they heard the words. One of them turned to him as the closest to a representative of the British government that there was in the room. "Can you make it out?" he shouted. "Can you understand these British fools? To turn down peace now? They're crazy!"

The atmosphere in the Foreign Office in London was similar. Many of the officials there strongly believed that Britain could not win the war, and that the peace offer should have been accepted at this late stage.

The following morning, in the House of Commons, the Labour MP for Ipswich demanded to know how Delmer – who he described as "a person of no importance" – should have been allowed to answer Hitler without Parliamentary authority.

But Duff Cooper backed the BBC. Delmer had spoken with the full authority of the cabinet, he lied. That same week, a new name was added to the secret list in Berlin of British people who should be arrested immediately after the invasion, the *Sonderfahndungsliste GB* (otherwise known at the infamous Black Book). Delmer should be handed over immediately to Dept. IV B.4 of the Central Reich Security Office.

By the beginning of the Battle of Britain, Goebbels and Newsome were learning from each other. The European Service quietly decided to exaggerate the odds against the RAF during the fighting, on the grounds that it wouldn't matter if they lost, but – if the British won – it would provide an important propaganda coup. It also became a matter of pride for the BBC to reply, over the air, to Goebbels' weekly column in the newspaper *Das Reich* within four hours of its appearance on the streets of Berlin.

But Goebbels was learning some lessons too. He was determined that people across Europe should not be in any doubt, because they had to wait for it, that the invasion of Britain would go ahead. It had to happen before people expected it rather than afterwards, he wrote. But as it became increasingly clear that this was not going to happen, Goebbels began to recognise the dangers of over-optimism. He called it "the irretrievable error of war-time propaganda".

Neville Chamberlain's government had developed a propaganda strategy which attempted to divide the Germans from the Nazis. Churchill rejected the idea and it was never really put into action, to Goebbels's relief. "Thank God the English didn't pursue this line," he wrote. Churchill rejected the idea of developing either a peace slogan or an elaboration of war aims, which made the task of the British propagandists even tougher.

When Hitler's speech of 4 September 1940 was broadcast all over Europe, he spoke directly to those in Britain who were wondering when 'he' was coming. "Keep calm," he said. "'He' will come all right."

Goebbels was exasperated, and not just with Hitler, for the delayed invasion. He was irritated by the failure of the British to respond to his propaganda. He complained how 'unEuropean' their mentality was. This was an interesting remark, because the nature of Europe – and Britain's place in it, if any – was precisely the issue behind the increasingly bitter arguments in the corridors of power between the BBC and Whitehall.

The new European Service, still under BBC control, was now gearing up. There was a five-fold increase in staff, and the latest transmitters were on the way from America, and suddenly the new headquarters of the European Service – a former ice rink in Delaware Road in Maida Vale – was becoming a centre for actors and journalists from across Europe, where they rubbed shoulders with the exiled governments and assorted propagandists from all over the British government machine. It was becoming a huge engine of European creativity.

But what was the role of broadcasters in the struggle for the hearts and minds in Europe? Could there be such a thing as 'white', or truthful propaganda?

This seems like a contradiction to the modern world: how can propaganda be moral, let alone truthful? The word reeks of compromise and official deceit. The whole idea of the BBC's involvement in 'propaganda' was been glossed over ever since – news, information, inspiration, entertainment, yes; propaganda, certainly not. But Newsome was developing a different approach to the news with what he called a 'moral' core. He also believed their bulletins should be recognisably British, and that the ideals for which they were fighting should shine through every broadcast – through religion, art, literature and the whole orchestra of free culture.

"So far we have merely scratched about on the surface, repeating arguments based on unprincipled and superficial ideas about the political, social and economic likes and dislikes of our audiences; scoring facile but impermanent victories," Newsome wrote in his 'propaganda plan' in July 1940, as the full scale of the task ahead sank in:

> "If our propaganda remains superficial, unprincipled and opportunist it cannot, however clever or cunning, contribute anything towards shortening the war, still less towards laying the foundations of a post war world fit for anyone to live in. It is not enough to show ourselves smart by exposing [lies] and the Nazis stupid by perpetrating them so clumsily. We must go much further and show that these frauds are the inevitable manifestations of a fraudulent system, of a system which is a fake to its very core, a hollow sham which by its very nature cannot endure..."

The British were to be portrayed as the ethical

victors: historically and morally they would survive. It was this approach which inspired the European Service, but infuriated Newsome's opponents inside the various government agencies tasked with projecting Britain's views to Europe. It infuriated the Left because it was too bombastic, and the Right because it was too objective. It worried the Foreign Office because they feared it implied postwar promises about the shape of Europe. Most of all, it infuriated officials who hated giving out information. And in the end, it infuriated the politicians who saw no role for Britain in postwar Europe, and who withdrew as quickly as they could into proud austerity and the Atlantic alliance the moment the war was over.

It also irritated the various national editors, who were developing their own tones. The French Service was beginning to show a possible way forward, waspish and witty. It was soon clear that the Nazi-controlled Radio Paris was appealing to the more educated French listeners, while the other end of the social scale seemed to be listening to the BBC news. Letters were arriving from listeners in France, sent via neutral countries: one of the peculiarities of the European Service was that, despite the closed borders, they received hundreds of letters from listeners – even from

Poland – every week.

The programmes were being heard, but otherwise there was a disturbing silence from the occupied nations. Until the Nazi advance in the early summer, they had been alive with debate, noise and resistance. Now, under the rule of invaders, the darkness was all but complete. Not a sound, apart from the letters and the bombastic twittering from the Nazi- or collaborator-controlled radio stations, disturbed the quiet. It was hard to know whether morale was so low that nothing was happening at all. If there was any kind of organised resistance, or any kind of belligerent spirit, left then there was little evidence of it.

It was the French broadcaster Maurice Schumann who decided to test the water, and asked people in France to stay at home between 2 and 3pm on New Year's Day 1941.

His 'stay-at-home' hour went ahead with great success. It hardly brought the nations to a standstill, but people responded. It was that discovery – that Europe might respond – that led to the V campaign that followed.

3
The V Campaign

"When the British government gives the word, the BBC will cause riots and destruction in every city in Europe."
Douglas Ritchie, 'Broadcasting as a weapon of war', paper written to BBC European Board, May 1941.

Douglas Ritchie was an unlikely military strategist. He had left his home in South London when he was grown up to try out farming in South Africa and drifted into journalism, before returning to join the staff of the pre-war *Daily Telegraph*. He was self-effacing and careful, but he was also determined. He was completely committed to truthful news, but fascinated by the potential for psychological warfare over the radio.

Over the period of Christmas 1940, he had begun to wonder what other uses broadcast news might be put in order to help the long process of liberation that lay ahead. He began writing a proposal for the Foreign Office, which then and later had the main influence over the BBC's

European operations, suggesting a plan to encourage active sabotage in occupied Europe. He was aware that Churchill's broadcast to France back in October had promised the occupied nations that "presently you will be able to weight the arm that strikes for you". It was a vague promise but it demanded consideration.

Ritchie was convinced that the myth of resistance might have to be fostered before anyone would have the nerve to start resisting. His paper put this case and argued that the most important message of his proposed broadcast campaign was that liberation would come – that much was certain; what was uncertain was *when*. Schumann's stay-at-home hour in the BBC French Service had been a huge success. They should build on that.

Silence followed. It was weeks later that their Foreign Office advisor sent Ritchie a message, via Newsome, that: "Ritchie might like to know that his paper is having a very fair wind." More silence followed.

One reason for the continuing silence would soon become clear, but in the meantime, something strange was happening. For some weeks at the end of 1940, Newsome and Ritchie had been getting reports of the slogan 'RAF' chalked as graffiti on walls in France and the Low Countries. Someone out there clearly wanted to show some kind of resistance, but what did the latest graffiti mean in January? It was just the single letter V, according to a Reuters report from Normandy. A memo around the various different language services soon provided the answer. It referred to an idea broadcast by the BBC Belgian Service.

Newsome and Ritchie went round to see them and their director, the ebullient and smiling Victor de Laveleye, editor of the Belgian Service, admitted that it had all been his idea.

De Laveleye was a former Belgian justice minister (and Olympic tennis player) who had escaped ahead of the invaders and was living in London, sharing a large dormitory with a group of Polish soldiers. A few months before, he had run into a British diplomat he knew who asked him if he might take charge of broadcasts to his own country. He was another good choice: he was always smiling, impossible to dislike.

De Laveleye had also noted the impact of the New Year's hour organised by de Gaulle and the Free French, and was aware that the graffiti 'RAF' was appearing on old buildings and derelict sites all over Brussels and other Belgian towns. So, on his own authority, on 14 January 1941, he suggested something simpler – the letter V.

He noted on the air that it was the first letter of the French word 'Victoire' and the Flemish 'Vrijheid'. It also happened to be his own initial letter. "The occupier, by seeing this sign, always the same, infinitely repeated, would understand that he is surrounded, encircled by an immense crowd of citizens eagerly awaiting his first moment of weakness, watching for his first failure," he said.

There were other possible places the original idea came from. One was an idea from the 'black' propaganda Nazi broadcasts to the UK in the early months of the war, via what they called the New British Broadcasting Service but broadcast from Berlin, which encouraged listeners to scrawl P for 'peace' on walls. At one stage, they were claiming someone had painted out the word 'Paddington' at the station, just leaving the P. It was never clear whether this was true or not. The satanist Aleister Crowley also claimed to have suggested the idea.

Wherever the inspiration came from, de Laveleye's V was catching on. It was already clear that people were taking his advice, not just in Belgium but in other countries where they heard his broadcast, in the Netherlands and northern France. In fact, he was rather proud of it. It was impossible to be cross with a man like de Laveleye, but Newsome was concerned. At least he should have known about it. There was in this, wrote Ritchie later, "the seeds of the huge dispute over news co-ordination."

The early weeks of 1941 had been, paradoxically, a moment of hope for Britain, still standing alone against Hitler's forces on the other side of the Channel. But, by the early Spring, it was clear that the situation had not changed. Britain's position remained perilous and there was hardly a squeak from the great darkness now covering most of Europe, except for the predictable voices from the previously friendly radio stations, now in the hands of Quislings and collaborators.

By March, Rommel was besieging Tobruk, and losses were mounting in the North Atlantic. Britain was clearly losing the war. They badly needed to make their case to Europe. What else was there to do?

The reason why Ritchie had received no proper reply to his paper on sabotage was that the news co-ordination row that was now escalating out of control.

In February 1941, after some trouble with the

Belgian government in exile over control of output, Churchill ruled: "In all questions of propaganda whether by broadcast or by the dropping of leaflets, the view of the recognised government should normally prevail." But he added that, where approved cabinet policy conflicted with the views of an allied government, then the Secretary of State would have the final word.

But which Secretary of State? Here was an even more fundamental argument: which senior politician would control the nation's propaganda, especially the messages to Germany? On the face of it, the man in charge was Duff Cooper, as Minister of Information. But he had visited the Delaware Road ice rink, where the European Service now perched, in such a black rage that it was clear he was not exactly getting his own way.

Then there was the Foreign Office, which controlled relations with the foreign governments in exile. There was also Hugh Dalton's new Ministry of Economic Warfare, with the remit from Churchill to "set Europe ablaze". Dalton was already in charge of the Special Operations Executive, which were in the process of recruiting Sefton Delmer to run their 'black' propaganda radio stations broadcasting to Germany. Around

Dalton clustered a range of trade unionists and young politicians and journalists on the Left, convinced that it would be possible to ferment revolution in occupied Europe and itching to try.

Then there was the complexity of the BBC and its layers of committees and sign-offs, which were next to impossible to comply with in the heat of the moment when Goebbels needed a reply. It was already clear to Newsome that one vital skill for anyone who wanted to shape convincing wartime news broadcasts was to encourage trust by getting your own bad news out before the other side.

The BBC was also bogged down in one of its own perpetual struggles with the government. As the darkness deepened through 1941, the BBC director-general Frederick Ogilvie and his committees, became increasingly defensive. When Robert Foot, general manager of the Gas, Light and Coke Company, was appointed to join the BBC to investigate their finances, nobody greeted him at Broadcasting House. Nobody even came to his new office to see him. On the dot of 11 am, the phone rang. It was the long-departed Lord Reith, urging Foot to sack Ogilvie.

Ironically, it was Foot's Coke Company which originally identified V as a piece of graffiti and arguably influenced de Laveleye. They had been painting white Vs on kerbstones across the capital to show where the gas valves were, and in such a way that they would be visible in a blackout.

Then there was the inflammatory issue of co-ordination. The foreign governments, quite naturally, wanted to control news and propaganda to their own people. Newsome wanted to co-ordinate the news across the different languages so that it was recognisably British, rather than apparently spun. The various departments of state wanted to co-ordinate Newsome.

Those around Dalton complained of "unco-ordinated excursions into Political Warfare". The situation was complicated by the unpopularity of Dalton, who would turn up at the Special Operations executive (SOE) headquarters at Woburn House on Sundays and force staff to accompany him on long country walks (it was his colleague Ernest Bevin who talked about Dalton's "concentrated gaze of unfathomable insincerity"). The real question was whether communications to continental Europe would be unified under the Ministry of Information, or whether it would be unified under the sabotage experts at the Ministry of Economic Warfare.

Harold Nicolson, the diarist, biographer and co-creator of the gardens at Sissinghurst Castle, was then despairing of his job as junior information minister. "Either we are responsible for the handling of news or we are not," he confided in his diary. "If we are not, we had better dissolve the ministry. If so, then we must have greater authority."

Nicolson was also a BBC governor and aware of the impact of BBC bureaucracy on Newsome and Ritchie's efforts. He met Newsome for a clandestine lunch early in 1941, and Newsome followed up with a meeting with both Nicolson and Duff Cooper himself. It was their suggestion that Ivone Kirkpatrick should be appointed as advisor to the European Service. "We'll give you Kirk," said Duff Cooper, according to Newsome. "He's a real terrier. He'll soon tear the pants off the BBC people."

Avuncular and with a small black moustache – not completely different from Hitler's – Kirkpatrick was a diplomat's diplomat, though he was then head of the Information Ministry's foreign department, and an expert on Germany. He had been Chamberlain's interpreter, much to Kirk's disgust, as he signed the Munich agreement in 1938. He was about to become the interrogator of Rudolf Hess, and, unlike his BBC predecessors, he was absolutely clear what he wanted. "Now, I'll just knock this out, and I'll knock that out," he would say gently to Whitehall officials, as he drew neat but definite lines through their draft propaganda directives.

This was the beginning of the small revolution in control of the European Services which made it possible for Newsome and then Ritchie to operate with the clarity and independence they needed to win the trust of their listeners. It was a shift that took most of the year to come to fruition, but – by the end of it – Kirkpatrick was in charge as 'controller'. He regarded his remit as protecting Newsome and Ritchie from the competing demands of the various rival ministries and, although the BBC was still paying their salaries and managing the new building – the old J. Walter Thompson headquarters of Bush House – they had slipped out of its bureaucratic grip.

This move was not a moment too soon: the Delaware Road studios took a direct hit a few weeks later.

The historian Michael Stenton explains that these were the foundations of the huge influence of an important institution. Newsome was, he said, "delighted that providence had called him to exorcise the moral cynicism which fed fascism and to teach a resumption of confidence in liberty. He wanted his European Service to sing with optimism about man and freedom. He did not doubt he had something to say".

It was Kirkpatrick and freedom from BBC control which allowed Newsome the independence he needed – not without controversy and certainly not without conflict with the propaganda chiefs and with his own language directors – but successfully. It also provided the glimmer of possibility for the V campaign to become a reality. It was a bid for independence which made the reputation of the postwar BBC, but which they never forgave.

By the end of April 1941, the administrative in-fighting had become impossible. The service departments were putting out press statements about the fighting in North Africa with minimal content. "Would you risk your life to listen to that?" Newsome would scrawl on mealy-mouthed rehashes of official communiqués. It was a frustrating time.

It was at this point Hess got into a Messerschmitt and flew to Britain for reasons which have never been entirely clear, though it seems to have had something to do with Hitler's imminent attack on Soviet Russia. Whatever the reasons, it brought the tensions in London around control of news to a head.

Kirkpatrick – the only Foreign Office official who had actually met him – was rushed to Scotland to question him. A bizarre official silence descended. As information minister, Duff Cooper begged Churchill to let him say something – anything. Goebbels himself was so nervous at the prospect of what the British would say on Hess's behalf that he claimed to be ill and stayed in bed in the country.

The German communiqué, which was changed by Hitler, explained that Hess had been suffering from a debilitating mental disease, and had managed to get hold of a plane and had left behind a letter which "unfortunately showed traces of a mental disturbance justifying the fear that he was a victim of hallucinations".

Their intention was not just to cast doubt on Hess' sanity in his quest, but to make the British distrust what he said. And in this they followed Hess' own instructions: he said that, if his mission failed, he should be described as mad. It said nothing about where he was going, in case he had never got there.

Goebbels first saw the text – which he claimed in his diary was the first he heard of the incident –

when it was sent to Berlin. If Hess was mad, Goebbels confided to himself, why had he been allowed to stay on as Hitler's deputy? "At the moment I can think of no way out. But one will be found," he wrote in his diary. "A fool like this was the Fuhrer's deputy. It is scarcely conceivable. His letters are littered with ill-digested occult theory... The whole thing can be traced to his mystic obsession with healthy living and all that nonsense about eating grass..."

The significance of the Hess affair for the V story is that it brought the propaganda disagreements to a head. It was the moment also when a frustrated Duff Cooper's health broke down and he disappeared to Bognor Regis to recuperate. When he recovered, he came back furiously demanding a seat in the war cabinet. Dalton was frustrated that his own sabotage plans were being blocked. Kirk was injured in a car accident shortly afterwards and was not at work. While the tensions inside government were reaching boiling point, it was clear, at least to Ritchie, that no answer to his proposal was likely from the Foreign Office for some time.

Yet Vs were still appearing and the French Service had done their own V broadcast in March. Now letters were beginning to filter into the BBC from listeners who had been inspired by it. One letter, also from Normandy, said that they had gone out and chalked Vs on the wall as soon as they had heard the programme. Newsome and Ritchie had begun to think about the potential of gestures like this: as yet, there was no link between the Vs appearing on walls in occupied Europe and Ritchie's sabotage proposals.

Ritchie went for advice to a friend among the radicals at the Ministry of Economic Warfare, and they agreed that he had made something of a tactical blunder. He had aimed too high. He decided instead to write a much more specific proposal to the BBC's European Board. He would call it 'Broadcasting as a weapon of war'.

Ritchie's new proposal borrowed from de Laveleye's V idea, and suggested taking the letter across the continent. It emphasised the simplicity of the idea and how easy it would be to take part in minor resistance. "At a word from London, railway lines all over Europe can be rendered temporarily unsafe by means of rocks and logs thrown on the metals," he wrote. "Telephone and telegraph lines can be cut." These would be negligible as individual acts but, taken together, they could be extremely disruptive. This would also do something to restore the morale among the occupied nations. The central idea was that there would be a "clear and co-ordinated policy in regard to what we want the oppressed people to do and how we should persuade them to do it".

The European Board loved the idea and responded immediately by proposing that Ritchie should chair a new group inside the BBC European Service staff called the Weapon of War Committee. It was formed two weeks later, as London underwent one of the worst nights of the blitz, the raid that destroyed the House of Commons chamber. It was the Scandinavian editor Roger Hinks who suggested calling it the V Committee. It was an important step forward.

The remit of the committee was to:

"(a) to create the frame of mind in which our listeners will feel themselves part of great army; (b) to give instructions to this army that will be good for its morale and bad for the morale of the German garrisons; and (c) to give suggestions and instructions to the Occupied Countries which will greatly increase Germany's economic difficulties."

Ritchie was a self-confessed 'worrier' and was nervous about chairing a committee of this kind.

He wrote out what he needed to say and consequently dominated the meeting, looking up nervously at Darsie Gillie, the former *Guardian* Paris correspondent, now French editor, to gauge what would inevitably be an aggressive reaction. He was allowed to take on a full-time committee secretary and the BBC chose the *New Statesman*'s drama editor John Palmer.

But Ritchie was right to worry about the governments-in-exile which were, equally inevitably, hostile to the idea. They wanted to be the ones giving the orders and shaping the propaganda. The solution was to bypass them by broadcasting in English.

The European Service was broadcasting by then in 25 different languages for a total of just over 25 hours a day, across three wavelengths. One of those wavelengths was in English, partly to cater for the English speakers across Europe and partly because the short wave English broadcasts were much more difficult to jam.

It was also a way of demonstrating that this was a recognisably British news network – which was the foundation stone of Newsome's approach. To be trusted, he believed, the news needed to be the same everywhere – different slants would only be exploited by the enemy – and it had to be clear and proud of where it was coming from. Too much sophisticated tailoring of messages, too much spin, simply spread distrust. This was the heart of the moral approach. The V committee agreed to make their appeals in English. That meant they needed a recognisable person to do it.

Ritchie wrote the script and took it to the head of European presentation, William Gibson Parker, to record. Parker suggested that Ritchie read it and, never having heard his recorded voice before, they were both delighted with the result. There was a quiet authority to it. Ritchie had, by his own confession, never given a speech to more than twelve people in his life before. He was now about to speak to millions, if they were listening.

But he needed a name. It was pointless using his own. There needed to be a military edge to it and the name needed to be obviously false – something like 'Colonel Great Britain'. But if he had the temerity to call himself 'Colonel Britain', especially as the broadcasts had not been agreed by any of the government departments in charge of them, he knew the world would fall on his head. But if he spelled it differently, perhaps it would still work – so Colonel Britton it was to be.

The V committee gathered to hear the recording and liked it. It was broadcast on Friday

6 June, just after midnight in Double British Summer Time, an hour behind continental Europe. It was the time most likely to catch the illicit listeners of Europe, bent quietly over the wireless sets in search of news.

The first official V broadcast was only four minutes long. There was no point in boring the audience, and it began with describing the letters from listeners arriving in London. Then it described a series of tiny acts of symbolic resistance, from travelling as much as possible and misusing official forms to saluting public clocks in the V position (five minutes past eleven).

Britton went on to discuss minor acts of resistance which anyone could do. It was more than just writing Vs on abandoned buildings: people could slow up at work. They could hide metal, hoard small change. They could not know the direction of anything when they were asked by foreign forces. The proposals were just suggestions, and they were hardly acts of terrorism. There was also a feature of all the V broadcasts, even in the first one – the injunction to be careful:

"Watch the Germans. Consider carefully what you can do and what you will do, but don't be in a hurry. If you want to deal an effective blow, the timing is extremely important."

They wanted to give a sense to occupied Europe that they still had power if only they knew it. They wanted to improve their morale, but there were enough voices urging caution from the various British agencies concerned with war information for Ritchie to be only too aware of the dangers. They must not give them the impression that any kind of liberation was coming any time soon. They must not encourage them to risk their lives and they must definitely not encourage any kind of insurrection that would make it more difficult to do so when the time for liberation came. They must not give the Nazis excuses to take reprisals against the civilian population. It was an example of what Ritchie called later "using the brake and the accelerator at the same time".

In the days that followed, most of the foreign language services took up their lead. "Chalk Vs are easy to rub out; Vs in indelible pencil are more difficult," said *Les Français Parlent aux Français*. "And in tar, even more so. There were some beauties in Nîmes just in front of the Hotel

Imperator." It was three days after the first broadcast that they discussed the implications of using the Morse Code signal for V (di-di-di da) – and Britton suggested summoning waiters by knocking on restaurant tables like that in a broadcast two weeks later. But it was John Rayner from SO1 (formerly of the *Daily Express*) who first knocked on the table of the V committee and pointed out that it was the first phrase of Beethoven's Fifth Symphony.

Ritchie was musical himself – he wrote music – and this inspired him. He experimented with recording the opening notes with two oboes and a trumpet to use as a call sign, but it proved just too distinctive for people who were listening to radios secretly. So they used a drum and the drum beat Morse Code V became a recognisable symbol of resistance over the course of the war, used widely on the BBC European broadcasts, as the signature tune to *Les Français parlent aux Français*.

Newsome had always believed in the power of culture. There would be no shunning of German composers as there had been in the First World War. Quite the reverse, the whole arsenal of European culture would be flung at the enemy, and the Morse letter V provided an opportunity to adopt the whole of Beethoven's Fifth Symphony as a kind of signature tune for the campaign.

Early in July, Radio Hilversum, under Nazi control, started broadcasting Beethoven's Fifth before an announcer came on suddenly to say it had been broadcast in error. Soon the symphony had disappeared from Axis run radio stations, but turned up oddly on Vatican Radio, but shorn of its 'di-di-di da' phrase at the beginning. Was this sitting on the fence or a subtle message of support from the Pope? It was hard to tell.

The Colonel Britton broadcasts were translated and read on the other language wavelengths. If the V campaign was an attempt to turn battered and defeated nations into resisters, then there was a clear impact on the divided French. "At the beginning, it was everything. We needed help from outside and the BBC gave that help," said André Philip, labour minister under de Gaulle's exiled government (Radio Paris used to call him the Minister of the Interior in the Exterior).

The essence of broadcast propaganda is to demonstrate your own on-the-stop knowledge. It unnerves your opponents and encourages your friends, and now the BBC French Service took up the challenge. This was their campaign song:

"Il ne faut pas

Désespérer
I'll ne faut pas
Vous arrêter
De résister!
N'oubliez pas
La letter V
Écrivez la!
Chantonnez la!
V! V! V! V!"

But there were by now strong signs that the campaign was working. The Vs were painted in tar on the sides of ships, in washing in sheets and clothes laid out in fields, chalked on the backs of German soldiers in cinemas, and on little bits of paper fluttering down from tall buildings. The letter was sounded out on car horns, factory hooters and tapped lazily by people waiting in queues. An RAF bomber dropping leaflets over Paris flashed the letter V at the ground and saw the answering flashes from car headlights below. Another RAF plane had the letter V flashed by a Norwegian fishing boat below in the North Sea at night. "Those imbeciles are tapping on wood in a certain way because London has ordered them to do so," said Norway's Quisling culture minister, Gulbrand Lunde.

The response was also immediate from inside the UK, where people were also able to receive the European Service broadcasts in English, where Newsome also began to broadcast in his own voice as 'The Man in the Street', to provide a co-ordinating line. There was an increasing audience for the idea of a V campaign. The UK papers were beginning to realise the attractions of Colonel Britton.

The cartoonist David Low suggested waspishly that V stood for vulgarity. Others hailed the 'Scarlet Pimpernel of the Radio'. Reporters tried to discover his identity. He wasn't in the phone book in London or in the Army List. MI5 claimed not to know who he was. Even the American magazine *Time* managed to trace the 76-year-old Colonel Reginald Brittan, formerly of the Sherwood Foresters regiment – but it wasn't him either.

Unnerved by the prospects that Colonel Britton would be unmasked, the authorities clamped down on the coverage. Fleet Street was not allowed to speculate on his identity.

Once the European Service had arrived at Bush House, the maze of corridors and lifts were filled with nationals from every country in Europe, from all the countries which Hitler had invaded. From the basement by the newsroom, Newsome and Ritchie now presided over a miniature Tower of Babel gathered around the microphones, with all the bizarre disadvantages and petty irritations which that entailed.

Sitting in the vast canteen in the basement, open round the clock, you could catch a glimpse of Jan Masaryk, who would later exit from the first post-war government of Czechoslovakia through a Prague window in 1948, probably at the hands of the communists.

Or of Patrick Gordon-Walker, later the man Harold Wilson appointed Foreign Secretary, doyen of the Political Warfare Executive. Or of James Bond's creator Ian Fleming, waiting impatiently for his broadcast in German. You would not have seen the great German novelist Thomas Mann – the exception to the rule that only non-Germans would be acceptable to German listeners – because his broadcasts were recorded at his home in California and relayed from the Bush House studios.

This was, after all, now the biggest broadcasting operation in the world. And drawing up in their taxis outside were an array of Europe's crowned, soon-to-be and almost crowned heads – General de Gaulle stooping out of the his car door, hotfoot from his headquarters in Carlton House Terrace. Generals Sikorski or Montgomery, ushered in with uniformed assistants. Even occasionally Winston Churchill himself, pondering his radio diatribe in awkward French. They would arrive along the wide streets leading to the Aldwych, with its boarded up shop windows covered with imaginative murals, along the white painted kerbs for the black-outs, the missing stumps which used to be iron railings, and the posters for Wills Capstan Cigarettes.

They would drive up the Strand, past the Lyons corner house and the trams on their way to the interchange in Kingsway, the traffic reduced by petrol rationing. Past the array of moving hats along the pavement – black helmets, shiny caps or homburgs for the men, jaunty angled creations for the women, with their shoulder pads and their hair pegged up and back, 1940s-style. Past Robertson Hare's name up in big letters at the Strand Theatre in the long, and probably rightly, forgotten play *Women Aren't Angels*.

Or from the other direction, perhaps, past the shell of St Clement Danes church, bombed six times in the Blitz - its Rector died of grief, they said - and on its blackened walls a poster shouting 'HIT BACK with WAR SAVINGS and STOP THIS'. Then on past the newly-built Gaiety Theatre and the

Aldwych underground station, where ENSA were playing concerts in the evening to entertain people sheltering from the raids. Or past the Aldwych Hotel, where senior European Service staff disappeared in the evenings for a quick drink, before returning to watch the hand over to the Night Shift at 8pm – keeping a weather eye open for the roof, where the Air Ministry flew a red flag when London was in 'immediate danger' from raids.

It was an exciting time to be in London. Outside Bush House, literary life was enjoying a rebirth in the pubs of Fitzrovia up the road, the West End was enjoying an explosion of night life, as bars, basement cabarets and all-night 'bottle parties' open for business to cater for the new demand. Inside, the European service was beaming their news, talks, music and later their strange messages – 'Benedictine is a sweet liqueur' or 'Is Napoleon's hat still at Perros-Guirec?' – via the Daventry transmitter into the ether.

Inside, the secretaries, typists and translators, actors, academics, dashed purposefully along the miles of corridor. The editorial meetings were convened twice a day at 11am and 5pm, the section heads sitting round their large wooden table with the blackout curtains behind them, and the news was chattering down the wires – from news agencies across Europe, or from the BBC's own listening outpost at Caversham, or from the British Press Reading Bureau, run by a diplomat out of a converted lavatory in Stockholm.

The German papers would arrive every morning from Portugal - swapped, it was said, for a pile of British newspapers, between two small planes on the tarmac at Lisbon airport.

There was the German service translating the script for the latest satirical soap opera, sympathetically following the experiences of a Berlin charwoman called Frau Wernicke, cynical propaganda official Kurt and his easily-led friend Willi. Goebbels own figures show the BBC had one million German listeners already – one of them the future Chancellor Konrad Adenauer. In the room next door, the French service preparing the next edition of *Trois Amis*, an increasingly popular discussion programme.

And at the heart of the whole operation, past the Central Desk updating the news broadcasts in every European language, was Newsome or Ritchie (they shared an office and, at one stage, shared a flat near Lord's cricket ground) – a map sellotaped to the wall behind them, a pipe on Newsome's desk, and a phone to his ear.

Clarity and speed were crucial to this operation. The news bulletins were due, decisions had to be made – and if necessary, authority had to be flouted to get the news on the air ahead of the Germans.

This close relationship between the two sides – only a thousand or so miles from each other – meant that the contempt they both felt for each other was tempered to some extent with a hint of admiration. For all his bluster about the English – "enormously stupid, unenlightened and primitive," he said – Goebbels, at least, knew that the BBC was becoming effective.

Since June 1940, the future housing minister Richard Crossman had been based at the SOE secret headquarters in Woburn Abbey's indoor riding school, occasionally venturing up to their official headquarters at Electra House, a few minutes' walk from Bush House on the Embankment. He was badgering for a desk at the European Service.

"Crossman would have liked to run British propaganda to Germany," wrote the historian and former propagandist Michael Balfour. "He not unreasonably supposed he was going to do so." But it was not quite as simple as that.

Crossman's reputation as a German specialist was not high at Bush House, where they called him 'Double Crossman' behind his back. There were also differences of interpretation over the likely direction Stalin would take. Would he deepen his understanding with the Nazis and enter the war on the German side, or would Hitler's need for oil and hatred for Bolshevism lead to the two fighting each other sooner or later? Nobody knew, of course, but there were whole encyclopaedias of pet theories competing across bars around the Aldwych.

Crossman thought that Molotov's presence in Berlin during the winter meant that the two dictators were getting closer together, and there was a chance to divide Hitler from his generals – though they probably shared his basic repugnance for the Soviet system. Newsome didn't agree that Hitler and Stalin were about to be bound into an alliance, quite the reverse.

Then on the morning of 22 June, just a fortnight into the V campaign, it became clear that Newsome had been right. It was he who took it upon himself to describe Stalin as a new 'ally', rather than as the mealy-mouthed 'co-belligerent' preferred by the Foreign Office. There was a moment of horror from the political establishment until Churchill repeated the word in the House of Commons.

It took three days for Stalin to emerge from his shock of betrayal by Hitler and to begin the Soviet resistance to invasion. One of the immediate effects was that there were demands from Moscow for sabotage in western Europe to take the intense pressure off the German advance eastwards. Another effect was that Radio Moscow took up the V campaign with enthusiasm. You can "not only see the V sign but hear it in the knock on the door, the whistles of railway engines, the pealing of church bells," they said.

A previously sceptical British establishment was also coming round to the V campaign. It was at least a strategy and something had to be done, especially if it was a simple gesture that would please the Russians. The V committee was keen to be more ambitious too, and the idea was to build on the success of de Gaulle's demonstrations of resistance in France – the manipulation of crowds on the street at set times.

Ritchie's plan was to make the French national day, 14 July, into a European day of resistance – to spread V across the whole continent. The Free French were planning to hold a demonstration in Paris that day, and it made sense to use that as the basis for a much more ambitious day of small actions and a demonstration of the potential strength of the V Army, if and when it was called upon to act.

The date was set and the preparations were made. The announcement was made the week before on 7 July, but it was already clear that not everybody was happy. De Gaulle was not pleased that his demonstration was being hijacked by the British. The other foreign governments – and particularly the Belgians and the Dutch – said they would not take part in an event timed to coincide with another country's national day. The Ministry of Information was unhappy. Reluctantly, Kirkpatrick told Ritchie that the 14 July V Day had to be cancelled.

This was not just inconvenient; it was also embarrassing. They had already announced the date of the event. How could they backtrack now without looking ridiculous? How could the V Army sound serious when they announced a postponement for a week?

Ritchie's idea was that they would simply postpone, and not explain the reason why. It would look mysterious and strategic. So 20 July it was and, this time, Kirkpatrick managed to get a message from Churchill himself which could be read out on air and translated into the foreign language services: "The V sign is the symbol of the unconquerable will of the people of the occupied territories and a portent of the fate awaiting the Nazi tyranny."

At midnight the night before the great day, Colonel Britton set out the purposes of the action the following day:

> "Tomorrow, Europe's invisible army of many millions will come into being. Mobilisation should be carried out with the greatest discipline. Enlistments are simple. You are asked to do two things. First, you take a vow at the earliest moment on Sunday to continue faithfully this fight the best way you can for your countries – independence and honour, and that of other nations enslaved by Nazi Germany. Secondly you are asked to take every opportunity this Sunday to demonstrate to the Germans the mobilisation of the V Army by putting Vs on walls everywhere you can and by beating out the V sound whenever you get the chance. Let V be splashed from one end of Europe to the other."

In the morning of 20 July, the European Service put out a press statement:

"In a broadcast at midnight last night, 'Col. Britton' declared: 'The V Army will act when the moment comes in such a way that the Germans will be powerless, but wait for the word... Declaring that mobilisation of the V Army had begun, 'Col. Britton' said: 'This is the moment when men and women throughout Europe are dedicating themselves to a continuation of the war against Germany. In a few minutes, there will be millions of V signs on walls, doors, and pavements throughout Europe. You may hear distant bugles sounding it, or, perhaps, train whistles'."

It was already clear that the Nazi occupiers were nervous about the whole idea of V. It was also clear that there would almost certainly be some response.

French holiday-makers had been ordered home from their beach resorts by 20 July, ostensibly so that they could be fortified. There had been special efforts to take down any posters in Paris with Vs painted in – and 6,200 people had been prosecuted for painting the letter. There had even been an 8pm curfew imposed in the western French town of Niort because there had been so much V graffiti. But it seems unlikely that any of the experts at the BBC, or any of the rival government departments in London, could have predicted what Goebbels would actually do.

4
Goebbels responds

*"What people are seeking is some small sign
showing that they belong to the community which
was founded in this struggle. Lo! This sign exists.
It is the sign V, the initial for the old call
'Viktoria'."*
Hans Fritzsche, Radio Berlin, July 1941

It was a case of when you can't beat them, join them. It was already clear that some kind of shift was going on in the Nazi propaganda department. Four days before, the German conductor Wilhelm Furtwängler had conducted a performance of Beethoven's Fifth on the German home service. In the days before 20 July, both Hilversum and Oslo broadcast Beethoven's opening bars, the call sign of the V campaign. Something was going on.

The next clue about what this was came on the day before. Hans Fritzsche at Radio Berlin talked about Colonel Britton, who he described as "apparently rather a dodderer" – the idea was, presumably, to identify him with another retired British colonel, Colonel Blimp – and then made an outrageous claim: "Not for the first time, the British have stolen a German slogan."

Radio Paris explained on the day itself. V actually stood for the old German word 'Viktoria', and it was all the idea of patriotic soldiers in France. The idea for a V campaign, they said, "first dawned in the mind of a little tank driver who decorated his vehicle with the V surrounded, with laurels and completed it with a swastika."

As the day dawned, Goebbels most dramatic coup was only too obvious. The V was theirs, and always had been. A Paris street was renamed 'Rue de la Victoire'. V streamers were erected outside all the main hotels in Oslo. In Amsterdam, the royal palace was decorated with a 30 foot V streamer. A huge V sign was erected on the Eiffel Tower.

Goebbels confided the truth to his diary:

"The enemy has made a 'V' … into his propaganda symbol in the occupied territories. Without any more ado, I have the symbol commandeered by us. Now we are using this 'V' ourselves and saying that it means a German victory. End of problem! I had given the matter a lot of thought, but I never would have dreamed that the solution would be so simple."

Was it a solution? Both Newsome and Ritchie were nervous about the implications, but their response was obvious. Colonel Britton said that the Nazi V really stood for *verboten* (forbidden), *verkehrt* (upside down) and *vergeltung* (revenge). Newsome's 'Man in the Street' broadcast put the British case, which was that the other side had been feeling the heat:

> "Soon, perhaps, the Germans will have to pretend that the letters RAF stand for the Luftwaffe and the Cross of Lorraine is a new type of swastika ... that there never was a Third Reich and that Hitler's war was a myth."

Even so, there was clearly confusion, and on both sides. The German Radio Bremen forgot the line enough to complain that it was "the English who started this V business, just as they started the war." In Holland, over the weeks that followed, pro-British groups used white Vs, while their pro-German opponents used orange Vs. In other parts of Europe, people used the graffiti 'V RAF' just to make sure.

As late as November, a letter arrived at Bush House from Spain signed by 'a Catalan chauffeur', which said something about the frustration:

"We have also up till now been marking Vs on the walls with chalk, but now those rotters the Falange who cannot invent but only copy, are painting Vs on all the pavements together with the swastika. So we now write three V.V.Vs. Do you think they will copy this too?"

By the following month, the pretence that V was a Nazi symbol had begun to dissipate. In August, German radio in English broadcast a report from Copenhagen. The correspondent said he had taken his paper and pencil 40 miles around the city, and recorded only two Vs – one on a mudguard of a car and one in a disused church.

A nervous Ministry of Information agreed with an equally nervous BBC hierarchy that they would not adopt the campaign for home listeners. Yet, because the English language broadcasts of the European Service could be heard in the UK, there was widespread identification with V. A huge V appeared soon afterwards on the outside of Leicester Town Hall. Heinz adapted the V as an advertising slogan; so did Watney's Beer. There were a range of similar applications, from V insurance to Victory over Indigestion.

There were downsides, and you can see why the authorities were nervous about adapting the V campaign for home audiences. The letters, still in the archives in Churchill College, Cambridge, reveal the dark underside of this kind of campaigning – letters of denunciation from English suburbs and inner cities about their neighbours: "Will you please watch Louise Robinson of *** Avenue, Manchester," ... "who will lead you to a right gang of scum in this vicinity." And so on. Once the authorities began encouraging denunciations abroad, the home audiences might start doing it at home.

But the campaign was also capturing audiences in the USA, still nominally neutral. Even in those days, Alastair Cook was broadcasting his Letters from America, and was reporting on the Vs over there. General Motors had manufactured a motor horn which sounded di-di-di da. Roosevelt's Republican rival Wendell Wilkie wore an ostentatious tie-pin shaped like a V.

But the biggest asset to the campaign was now Churchill himself. Having backed the campaign on the airwaves, he now took to using a V sign on every public appearance – initially as a rude gesture and then, having been informed what it meant, the more familiar way round with the thumb at the front. Popular mythology suggests that the rude V sign was a mistake on Churchill's part. This is not completely clear: the sheer powerlessness of the resistance movement in Europe, and the defeated governments in exile in London, suggests that part of the appeal of the V was its simple rudeness. It was a gesture of defiance to Nazi rule. Either way, Churchill continued to use V signs with his fingers in public for the rest of his life (so did de Gaulle). It became his distinctive political trademark – it meant, not just eventual victory, but defiance in defeat.

That was the power of the campaign that V had become. It also implied its main weakness. Campaigning, white propaganda might never be decisive. When the BBC made a great deal of the Atlantic Charter, signed by Churchill and Roosevelt in August 1941, Goebbels replied:

"We don't want to win the war by propaganda. We have the German armed forces and we can afford to take the propaganda front lightly."

He may have been right, in the strict sense, but the success of the European Service, and the efforts of the V campaign, suggest that providing people with trustworthy information about the war was in itself a powerful and inspiring weapon. In that respect, Goebbels' reply was also an admission of defeat in his chosen sphere of pre-eminence.

In the summer of 1941, the military war was reaching some kind of crisis. There was bitter fighting in Russia as the German troops raced to seize Moscow ahead of the winter. In Crete and North Africa and the Atlantic shipping lanes, fighting was intense.

In the light of these conflagrations, the smaller battle in Whitehall over control of propaganda was also coming to a head. As advised by Lord Reith, Ogilvie was ousted as director-general, to be replaced by his private sector advisor, Robert Foot.

The stalemate was resolved by the arrival of a brilliant political operator, Churchill's red-haired friend Brendan Bracken, at the Ministry of Information which led to some kind of resolution. When Duff Cooper was sent as an emissary to Singapore, and Bracken moved in, he turned out to be the only Information Minister to make any kind of success of the role.

Thanks to a report by the Home Secretary Sir John Anderson – of Anderson Shelters fame – propaganda would now be decided by a triumvirate of departments: the Foreign Office, which delegated its role to Kirkpatrick, Bracken at Information, and it would have been Dalton at Economic Warfare – but Dalton was also out. In charge of Dalton's trade unionists and would-be revolutionaries was now the Tory Lord Selborne, who shared the establishment's suspicion of appeals to sabotage. In any case, Bracken had been too clever for Dalton, and by the end of the year he had virtual control over the propagandists. Sweeping away the maze of committees, Bracken suspended the BBC's charter for European broadcasting, and set up the Political Warfare Executive, known to history as PWE, to co-ordinate black and white propaganda.

This also allowed Kirkpatrick to consolidate his hold over European broadcasting. He was made controller, and used to sleep curled up on the table in his office at Bush House – regarding his role primarily as high-level protection for Newsome (the new 'director' of European broadcasts) and Ritchie as his assistant director. He invited them both in to see him, explaining that the BBC would no longer have a role in the operation – except to pay their salaries. The policies for broadcasting would now be decided by the PWE, which would share Bush House – but *how* to put those policies into action in practice, well, that was up to the three of them.

This also meant that the BBC's V committee would be wound up and replaced by a PWE V committee, which would be chaired by Robert Bruce-Lockhart. The final meeting of the V committee chaired by Ritchie took place on 1 October. The first meeting of the new committee took place shortly afterwards at the PWE's temporary headquarters in Berkeley Square. Bruce-Lockhart advanced on Ritchie, arm outstretched. "So you're Colonel Britton," he said.

Bruce-Lockhart had a formidable reputation as an intelligence officer. As a young man in Russia, he had actually been condemned to death by Lenin, only to be exchanged for Litvinov (his book *Memoirs of a Secret Agent* had already been made into a film). Despite his co-ordination role, and the authority of his job title – director-general – he would need every ounce of personality to control Crossman and the rest of his staff, not to mention his influence over the European Service. He had the main requirement – absolutely ferocious charm – but it wasn't quite enough.

The arrival of the PWE meant that the struggle to shape the message to Europe was now complicated by the new language editors inside the European Service and also the new heads for each nation at PWE. At the former BBC European Service, Darsie Gillie for the French service and Hugh Greene for the German service, were both sceptical about Newsome's approach and the V campaign, and both were demanding more independence. Crossman was struggling to get his own messages across and now there was also the former *Daily Herald* science correspondent Ritchie Calder in charge of the day to day operation, smoothing ruffled feathers and building trust. Kirkpatrick's assistant, the former announcer Harman Grisewood, remembered operating in what he called a 'no-man's land' between Newsome's 'radical fervour' and PWE's preference for subtlety and said he found the spectacle "edifying" and "moving".

This was not a point of view shared by colleagues in PWE who found it frustrating and infuriating. But Kirkpatrick believed that Newsome was right that, to build trust, the news had to be not just true but recognisably British. Too much subtlety and spin was counter-productive. So he protected Newsome and then Ritchie's right to direct. When PWE got particularly cross and demanded to see scripts or daily directives in advance, he simply failed to pass them on. Bruce-Lockhart's team was reduced to looking them up in the BBC archives. The PWE's official history described this as "Mr Newsome's insubordination."

This all seems unimportant now, but the huge success of the European broadcasts – not so much in capturing the imagination of occupied Europe – but of instilling trust when there was none before, even in Germany, suggests that he was right. In fact, it was Kirkpatrick, Newsome and Ritchie's ability to disobey orders which partly led to the huge reputation the BBC amassed during the war for trust. This has remained a potent legacy to this day.

It was time for the V campaign to gear itself up. Despite the scepticism of the propaganda hierarchy, it was almost the only medium available now for effective 'white' propaganda, and campaigning, to occupied Europe, and it was working – Goebbels' panicky adoption of the V himself showed that. Now, with the V committee chaired by PWE, they were keen to keep up the momentum. It was time for a Go Slow campaign.

The campaign recognised that there were now three million foreign workers who had been deported to work in German factories. If they could be persuaded to work just a little bit slower, and to take a little less pride in their work – and maybe even to draw some pride in their reluctance to work hard – it could make as much effect as a number of destructive bombing raids. It was announced on 15 August and set for 15 September, the anniversary of the biggest Luftwaffe losses in the Battle of Britain the previous year.

Colonel Britton was as careful as usual not to incite too much. Go Slow is "only a foretaste, a drill for other more resolute collective action, when the time comes," he said. This was a campaign that revealed the continuing influence of Dalton's revolutionaries and it was announced by Britton and the former trade unionist Ernest Bevin, who explained it like this:

"The British will work hard, you work slow, and together we will win."

It was clear very quickly that someone was responding. Reports came through of factories closing down after minor acts of sabotage, or trains which had been derailed, and even a strike in a Danish power plant. There was also a sudden interest in labour productivity on German radio.

There were reports of pictures of tortoises chalked on the walls of factories. But there was even evidence that the message was getting through from broadcasts from Moscow. If all the workers in Germany and wasted a minute in the rifle assembly lines, production would be reduced by enough to equip four divisions, said Moscow radio. Half a minute lost by miners would deprive five bombers of fuel to carry them to London. They were all figures which had come from Colonel Britton.

Bevin was the first of a number of leading politicians who were introduced to the microphone by Colonel Britton. The Greek prime minister in exile Emmanouil Tsouderos spoke; so did President Edvard Beneš of Czechoslovakia and Roosevelt's emissary Averell Harriman, and the future Chancellor Sir Stafford Cripps (his broadcast survives and can be heard online, introduced by Colonel Britton at http://www.bbc.co.uk/archive/ussr/6705.shtml)

Then, as the disastrous year of 1941 gave way to 1942, came the Rat Campaign, beginning with a quotation from Churchill's speech: "Particular punishment must be reserved for the quislings and the traitors. They will be handed over to the judgment of their fellow countrymen." Colonel

Britton promised to name and shame some of the 'rats'.

"We know the leaders," he said. "We know Quisling, Mussert, Darlan, Degrelle, Pavelitch, Moravetz, Filov and the others. We must know the smaller traitors, those who do dishonour to the name of rat. They are playing a dangerous game, these people. More dangerous than some of them think." The first rat was Ferdonnet, the former doyen of Radio Stuttgart, who was credited with such a bitter impact on French morale in 1940:

"Mr Ferdonnet, traitor of Stuttgart, are you listening? Do you think you're not known now that you've changed your name to Mouton? Do you think we were not watching you when you drank a toast to 'Chancellor Hitler' at that dinner in Paris?"

It was dangerous stuff, but exciting to hear. One Belgian captain who had offered to help RAF officers escape, but had betrayed them for 2,000 francs, was denounced as a rat. Another Belgian was named soon afterwards:

"And here's another rat for you. His name is De Cuypere—d-e C-U-Y-P-E-R-E, and his address is Villa Vroegezonne, Avenue du Littoral, Le Zoete. De Cuypere will regret that he betrayed the sailors. I would like to remind him that twice in a week British forces have visited the coast of Norway in order to wipe out a German garrison. When they came away last Saturday, they brought back to Britain nine little quislings. Nine little rats like you, Mr de Cuypere, who also live on the coast. You'd better think about this. We've long arms as well as sharp eyes..."

De Cuypere moved shortly afterwards. There was particular attention paid to the functionaries of the Vichy government:

"I was going to ask you to put on your blacklists the name of Paringaux, chef du cabinet to the French Minister of the Interior, Mr Pucheu. But, Paringaux has already learned that treachery is not so profitable as he thought it was, and his master, Pucheu, is very frightened. As you know, Paringaux was found a few days ago on a railway line, dead. Mr Pucheu, you are right to feel nervous. Quite right; your name is high up on the list!"

On 23 January, the first part of the weekly V talk concerned Alexander von Falkenhausen, German military commander in Belgium and the North of France as far as the Somme:

"This man plays a part. He pretends to be the nice and considerate general of 'the old school'. He ... likes to spread the belief that, if only he and other 'nice' generals were in control, everything would be all right. I know that he has even made uncomplimentary remarks about Hitler when Belgians were present. Don't be deceived by this. Falkenhausen is only an agent provocateur... His amiability is a mask. It doesn't stop him from putting his signature under scores of death warrants... This man betrayed the German conservatives to the Nazis. He betrayed his fellow generals. He betrayed Chiang Kai-shek, who trusted him as a friend and adviser. Don't let him betray you!"

Partly, no doubt, because of the rat broadcasts, Colonel Britton had gathered around himself an aura of power and influence. The UK press were not allowed to speculate about his identity, but the foreign press were fascinated. It made sense to encourage this atmosphere, but how could he be interviewed when Ritchie hardly looked the military type?

On one occasion, he therefore gave an interview behind a partition. On another occasion, he had to rule out photographs altogether. "Would you please tell *Illustrated*," Ritchie wrote to the BBC publicity department, "that Colonel Britton is a very shy bird indeed and will not hear of the suggestion that the back of his head should be photographed." Later, he gave this reply to a question about his previous career from United Press:

"I hope you'll forgive me if I ask to be excused from answering this last one – which is about campaigns which are past and done with. Let the dead past bury its dead."

The only insights that went beyond this came in the profile written in October 1941 by Joe Liebling of the *New Yorker*, who became a close friend of Ritchie's, so they may have actually met face to face. He certainly implies that they had dinner together.

Liebling's article 'Colonel Britton and the rhythm' is a fascinating glimpse by a nation still at peace into the wartime struggle. It was also a professional journalist's view of that corner of the Second World War that was being fought by and between journalists. He points out the huge power of the V campaign, explaining that it "probably costs less than the advertising of the average American toothpaste manufacturer." He described how the Colonel broadcast from what he called "a dismal little studio about the size of a hotel bathroom".

Despite David Low's V for Vulgarity jibe, Liebling suggested that "the V has caught peoples imagination in Britain; it gives them a feeling that luck is on their side, and that is not a bad feeling for a fighter to have. It is the first effective counterpart of the swastika."

He described listening to the Colonel Britton scripts being broadcast in Serbo-Croat to Yugoslavia, enjoying the fact that his name was rendered as '*Pukonyik Britonia*'. There was something of Professor Moriarty about Colonel Britton, he said, which "adds considerably to the juvenile charm which the British people find in the whole procedure".

But some of the new PWE officials were immune to juvenile charm. In particular, David Garnett, who was a minor figure in the Bloomsbury literary world, whose marriage in

1942 to Vanessa Bell's illegitimate daughter Angelica rather undermined his reputation, thanks to her memoir *Deceived With Kindness*. Garnett had been appointed as a secretary to the new V committee, with a remit to record PWE's activities for posterity. He did this immediately after the war, but in such an outspoken way that his book-length report remained classified as secret until 1980. Garnett found the whole procedure juvenile, partly because he believed neither Ritchie nor Newsome should be initiated into the secret world of high-level propaganda decisions. "The dangers of the Colonel Britton broadcasts," he said:

> "... were clearly realised in PWE, but as all of them were not, or perhaps could not, be clearly explained, Colonel Britton himself and his assistants in the BBC were frequently given the impression that they were being muzzled by a political warfare department which had not realised the potentialities of political warfare as well as he had himself...."

PWE was also co-ordinating the activities of Woburn Abbey, which included SO1 (black propaganda radio stations, now controlled by Sefton Delmer) and SO2, the agency now concerned with dropping agents into occupied territories. At the time Ritchie had proposed the V campaign, said Garnett later, "the BBC was not controlled by SO1 and the persons to whom he circulated his paper were ignorant of the existence of many secret SO1 activities and for that matter entirely ignorant of the existence of SO2."

What must have frustrated Garnett and those even more patronising than he was, was that Newsome and Ritchie – protected by Kirkpatrick and the might of the Foreign Office – were actually making things happen. They remained the only obvious success story and the flood of letters from occupied Europe into Bush House was testament that they were having an influence. But there did begin to be difficulties over V tactics. Special instructions were given for the celebration of Hitler's 53rd birthday. The V army was told to do its best to make this birthday a holiday all over Europe, and specifically to do three things:

1. Stay away from work on Monday.

2. Write as many letters as you can and post them on Monday.

3. Make as many telephone calls as possible on Monday, and make a point of telephoning at exactly 5pm.

That was fine and fun as far as it went, but did it amount to anything more? Garnett and Ritchie had a furious row some weeks later over an instruction to the V army to refrain from travelling on a Tuesday. Why Tuesday, asked Garnett? Why not travel? It wasn't clear. Ritchie admitted later that Garnett was probably right on this.

The real problem was that, for getting on for eleven months, the V campaign had repeated its mantra – "do the little things that waste time and materials, but no active sabotage yet" – but Europe had moved on. The reprisals were increasingly brutal, the various occupations increasingly tyrannical, and what's more the campaign had succeeded in its main objective. There was now a body of people in these territories who had recovered their morale and were prepared to resist. They now needed something more ambitious.

The Free French were discussing holding a general strike to protest at the murder of 50 civilians as a reprisal for the killing of a German soldier. De Gaulle had fallen out with SOE and with the emerging resistance movement in France over just these issues. The war was developing.

British policy-makers had been desperately concerned not to promise too much, or to encourage uprisings when they were in no position to support them. The experience of the naval raid on the Lofoten Islands in March 1941 was scorched onto their memories. The Norwegian residents had risen in revolt, only to face terrible reprisals afterwards.

Then there was the familiar argument, among the sophisticated political campaigners at PWE, that broadcasts to Europe as a whole were not of interest to individual countries. Greece was always used as an example. This enraged Ritchie – the idea of a sense of pan-European destiny was necessary to those who ran the European Service and would be controversial as soon as the war was over. "Surely Greece is not so parish minded that it is impossible to tell them anything about the rest of Europe?" he said.

What was definitely a problem was that the nature of the occupation was now different in different countries. It remained comparatively mild in Denmark, for example, but in Czechoslovakia, the Czech editor Shiela Grant Duff – who later married Newsome – decided to broadcast a direct appeal to the Nazis there to stop the reprisals after the assassination of Reinhard Heydrich. As for Poland, that was brutality on another scale. Even within the countries, there were difficult and complicated circles to square: in Croatia, for example, the BBC was attacked for being 'the voice of the Serbs'.

In February 1942, with Calder in charge of the V committee, PWE withdrew its objections to urging sabotage, as long as the governments in exile were consulted. But the truth was that any kind of invasion of Europe was still at least a year away and Britton's combination of accelerator and brake would have to continue for the time being.

Nor did Whitehall's nervousness go away as a result. PWE was worried about the impact of instructions for sabotage might have on IRA sympathisers in the UK. Maybe they might take it into their heads to try a little sabotage too. There was nervousness that a service nominally controlled by the BBC was urging people to blow up trains with the kind of atmosphere that they might urge people to collect silver paper or bottle tops. Should 'Auntie' be advocating terrorism?

There was also nervousness in Conservative circles about Bevin's broadcastabout going slow at work and the whole idea of calling for strikes. What if their own railwaymen responded? What if the idea of a Europe-wide trade union struggle took hold and involved British miners, for example? Many of the old hands in the UK security services regarded British railway unions with deep suspicion. And how dare a mere colonel take it upon himself to threaten senior foreigners? There was something about the knit-your-own revolution of Colonel Britton that unnerved the British establishment. They may be Nazi authority figures, after all, but if you start urging people to tear them down, well, anything might happen...

There were mistakes as well, which were seized on by Garnett and the other critics inside the PWE. The V campaign had been adapted for Dutch listeners, urging farmers to employ an extra labourer so that there would be one less civilian deported to the arms factories in Germany. But, in fact, the number of labourers allowed was based on the acreage of Dutch farms, and so the campaign merely revealed the ignorance of the campaigners about local conditions – the precise opposite of what was intended.

At least two of the 'rats' named also led to unforeseen consequences. The Quisling police chief in Blankenberge in Flanders purged his own police force as a result, and provided himself with a trusted bodyguard, which proved to be an inconvenience.

As for Nicole Bordeaux, named as the mistress of the German ambassador to Vichy, Otto Abetz, that led to a libel action by an enraged UK relative and angry questions in the House of Commons.

When it came to the idea of encouraging UK citizens to send messages to occupied territories by toy balloon, PWE officials stepped in and squashed the idea. It would interfere with their own plans for sending 'black' propaganda newspapers that way and, anyway, it might lead to "private un-co-ordinated propaganda".

The danger with not clearing the V campaign scripts with PWE was that sometimes claims that could be used against the allies managed to creep in. On one occasion, early in 1942, Colonel Britton talked about the Russian front, and said: "Within six weeks from now, there will be what may prove to be the greatest battle in the history of the world". SOE complained to PWE. "No disciplinary action was taken," wrote Garnett, disapprovingly.

As the disagreements intensified, Ritchie offered to end his own broadcasts on condition they were replaced by something equally ambitious and pro-active. But as it turned out, the officials at the Ministry of Economic Warfare and at MI6 and SOE had become fond of Colonel Britton, so for the time being, the V campaign carried on.

But the basic contradictions about the V

campaign, the different stages of development of both Nazi rule and resistance to it, were now becoming more intense. In May, Bruce-Lockhart wrote to Ritchie explaining that the broadcasts must end. The nervousness of the authorities about the repression that might follow sabotage at the wrong time had finally got the better of them. Bruce-Lockhart congratulated him on "capturing the admiration of the whole world and which I understand was mainly your own idea."

Ritchie was furious. He responded with a paper to the Foreign Office ('Britain's Right to Speak'), and complained about officials who "become more concerned with ... what they think our listeners want to hear than they are with what they want to say ... perhaps fearful that listeners will become angry or bored or switch off. They do not give sufficient weight to the other side, that if our listeners are not hearing what we want them to hear, it is not worthwhile broadcasting to them and that, in any case, our broadcasting has today in wartime a compelling interest for Europe and that the people who are opposed to Nazism (the great majority) *must* listen to us, directly or indirectly."

This was a powerful point, recognisable to anyone involved in political campaigning before or since. If you become so concerned with what other people want to hear that you forget what you want to say – as politicians so often do – then, really, what's the point? And as Ritchie said, since Britain was then prosecuting the war in western Europe, of course people wanted to hear what they had to say – whether they liked it or not. It was an extraordinary opportunity which, despite furious opposition inside and outside, the European Service largely grasped.

Losing Colonel Britton and V was a blow for Douglas Ritchie. He wrote sadly to Kirkpatrick, asking "whether anything can be done to save from extinction the 'V' campaign ... [the PWE], while professing that they had no wish to kill the campaign have, in fact, done their best to kill it."

But the truth was that the responsibility had also weighed heavily on him. "In his favour was the fact that hundreds and thousands of men and women were ready to risk death at a word," Liebling had written in the *New Yorker,* "but against him was the certainty that, unsupported by anything but words, those people would die in vain." On the other hand, he felt he had made promises to his listeners that he wanted to fulfil.

There were complaints from occupied Czechoslovakia immediately the broadcasts stopped. There was even a complaint from the shadowy C at the heart of MI6, actually Stewart Menzies. The official response was always that the V committee would be replaced. But the idea of launching a new committee to propose sabotage schemes caused so much internal argument – especially from the governments in exile – that the idea was abandoned.

What finally emerged in June was a PWE Committee on Operational Propaganda, the job of which was to organise a pan-European campaign to encourage people to waste fuel and disrupt transport, backed now by RAF raids. There were the usual arguments about whether Colonel Britton should be reinstated to introduce Sir Arthur Harris of Bomber Command to explain the background.

In the event, Crossman at PWE wrote his own script for Harris to read, to inform German listeners about the bombing campaign that was due to begin. He carried on the by now usual tradition of failing to get it agreed, and then broadcast Harris' talk a day too early, including the aggressive phrase: "You have no chance. Soon we shall be coming every night and every day."

Much more problematic, he included the idea that, all the German people needed to do to end the bombing was to overthrow Hitler. The cabinet was so cross that they demanded an inquiry, but Crossman was forgiven.

At the same time, the European Service was launching their own 'peasants' campaign', for people working on land, broadcast at dawn in twenty languages. As usual, PWE asked to see the scripts and Kirkpatrick protected his broadcasters by failing to pass on their requests.

But the success of the original campaign was clear. A few weeks after V came to an end, on 14 July 1942, the French Service urged people to show the French flag at windows at a set moment that day and to go into their town centres. Aerial photos by the RAF showed the massive response. In one street in Lyons, the crowds had so unnerved the Nazis that they had opened fire. In celebration, the BBC programme *La France Libre* was changed permanently to *La France Combattre*.

It may have seemed a purely symbolic gesture, but it showed how far the V campaign, and the European Service, had come. Occupied Europe was coming back to life. Soon there would be regular broadcasts to resistance members, copy for underground newspapers, twice daily broadcasts designed for deported forced labour in Germany. Newsome was to meet people in Germany after the war who told him they had found the broadcasts inspiring. It was, in fact, far more effective than mere symbolism after all.

5

Towards a European culture

"Boom! Why did my ship go boom?
Me and my ship go boom, boom-di-di-boom,
And founder?
Boom! When there're those U-boats bloom,
Out of the gloom,
And boom, boom-di-di-boom
Oh, I'm sinking!"
Charlie and his orchestra, Nazi propaganda
broadcast in English, 1942 (see book by
Bergmaier and Lotz in the bibliography).

It was an important element of Nazi cultural belief that jazz music was 'degenerate'. It had been banned on German radio. But Goebbels had been pushing for more relaxing music on their broadcasts, especially when they were fighting for listeners with American programmes made in their great broadcast factory in Santa Monica and shipped out to their invading forces. Also there were no reasons why the Nazi propaganda stations shouldn't use jazz as a weapon if they wanted to. The result was Charlie and his Orchestra, the Nazi response to the jazz revolution.

There were always difficulties with it, because jazz musicians were not biddable in the way the broadcasters wanted them to be. A drunken incident at a Berlin restaurant began with the trumpeter playing Yiddish songs and ended with him being carted off to a concentration camp.

Charlie was Karl Schwedler, the son of a plumber from Duisburg, who was the vocalist, and his propaganda orchestra played on a programme called *Political Cabaret*, broadcast on short wave to the USA from 1940 onwards. The BBC listening station in Caversham took down verbatim a parody of *Lambeth Walk* ("Clap their hands and swing it,/Germans also sing it...").

As the war went on, a desperation started to permeate the propaganda efforts of their own Nazi broadcasters, there was a new seriousness about the charge of listening to foreign broadcasts, as if it was the source of corruption. Had not the French succumbed so quickly because of the skilful broadcasts of Radio Strasbourg? Might not the same thing happen in Berlin or Munich? The Nazi ideology was built on the foundations of propaganda – of course it was effective.

But at the same time, black propaganda radio stations, pretending to be something they were not, were increasingly available at every turn of the dial – British broadcasters pretending to be German Catholics or disaffected U-boat crews, German broadcasters pretending to be Welsh nationalists.

There was Radio Caledonia, a Nazi radio station, providing news from a Scottish nationalist perspective. There was Worker's Challenge, also providing far left propaganda written in Berlin, but pretending to be broadcasting from a secret location in the UK. There was Gustav Siegfried Eins, a fake British radio station broadcasting to occupied Europe – controlled by Sefton Delmer – pretending to be a group of ultra-conservative anti-Nazi generals. There was Christian Peace Movement Radio, a Nazi radio station broadcasting to Britain, purporting to be organised by a secret cell of pacifists.

There was Radio G8 or Christ the King, a fake radio station run by the British in German which hinted strongly that it was controlled by the Vatican. There was Twelve Twelve, an American radio station using the Radio Luxembourg transmitter at the end of the war, giving misleading instructions to the German population on familiar wavelengths.

Then there were the radio stations which *were* what they seemed to be: Radio Paris, furiously anti-British, shaping news from the point of view of the Parisian intelligentsia which had made an accommodation with their German occupiers. There was also the New British Broadcasting Service, broadcasting from Berlin in English, written largely by William Joyce (Lord Haw Haw), and purporting to be an independent British point of view.

By the end of the war, there were also more than 300 American forces radio stations all over Europe, including the US Fifth Army Mobile Radio Station, broadcasting from wherever General Mark Clark happened to be. And of course there was Axis Sally (actually Mildred Gellars from Ohio) whose speciality was frightening American troops over the radio. Not for more than half a century would so much be available for listening on a simple wireless.

It was all there if you had the will – and in even in Germany, people did – especially to news they could trust amongst the cacophony. It was after all, a small act of resistance. You could listen to the radio, ignoring the legal warning on the dial, and put a pillow over your head as you did so and nobody would hear. Increasingly, the German Service of the BBC was also gaining listeners. You could hear lists of crewmen picked up after sinkings, lists of those who were prisoners of war. Maybe you could even hear their voices (the breakthrough by the German Service came in 1941 when they listed survivors from the sinking of the *Bismarck*). You could hear jazz (not on the European Service but on the American forces radio stations like AFN). You could hear religious services in German and concerts of German music.

One of the winning ideas was suggested by a junior member of the European Service staff, the future populariser of the Theatre of the Absurd, Martin Esslin, who suggested recording the bombastic speeches of the Nazi leaders to be replayed later. This wasn't simple; most recording discs – as they used then – were manufactured in Holland, which was under Nazi occupation. But it did lead to the European Service propaganda coup when the German Sixth Army had surrendered outside Stalingrad. They were then able to broadcast Hitler's speech which predicted that this would never happen.

But the heart of the British success was the appeal to authenticity, and an understanding that any effective political campaign required it. Here was the source of friction inside the European Service and, if Ritchie was self-effacing and reserved, Newsome was aggressive and combative. He combined a boxing blue with a first from Oxford. His talks editor, the historian Alan Bullock, complained later that he erred too far in the direction of the boxer. It was hardly surprising that he fell out with PWE, but he extended his critique to what he regarded as the dishonest reticence – or was it the stiff upper lip – of the establishment, which he regarded as the direct opposite of what being British was all about.

"We're British people, with all their qualities and faults, with feelings and emotions," he told his 500 staff after the fall of Singapore, "and not denationalised, impersonal polyglot cynics with the generous emotions of a fish, intimidated by fears that what we feel like saying will be 'bad propaganda'."

None of this went down at all well if you were a mandarin with fish-like emotions, and it required courage to broadcast the pain of defeat. But prisoners of war listening in the UK said that it seemed to them to reveal enormous confidence by being able to admit it.

By 1945, the BBC believed that 15 million Germans were listening regularly, and risking their lives to do so. By then, many thousands of Germans had been imprisoned, and many put to death, for listening to the radio. Faced with an unprecedented cacophony of the airwaves – unprecedented for them, and even for generations that came later until the age of the internet and digital radio – they chose to listen.

The consequences were bizarre. Like the Essen man in July 1941 who denounced himself for listening to foreign broadcasts, after his wife accused him of it in the hearing of the neighbours. Or like the family who went through with a proxy funeral for their son, a U-boat sailor, after he was posted missing presumed dead, even though they knew from BBC that was actually alive and a prisoner.

There was a more serious incident shortly after D-Day when a German junior military commander in France was arrested after his pep talk to his men, explaining what the military situation was. "How do you know that," shouted an obsessive Nazi from the back. "It hasn't been announced!"

These incidents were a measure of influence of the European Service. "There is one way in which the British, despite the narrowness of their political thinking, are ahead of us," Goebbels warned in a newspaper article in 1944. "They know that news can be a weapon and are experts in its strategy."

Goebbels' problem, as he recognised himself, was that he was not able to win the moral battle. "History is the propaganda of the victors," said the playwright Ernst Toller. That is true, but Goebbels' anti-semitism and involvement in the Holocaust meant he never had the moral high ground, even when he was dealing with the brutality of Stalin and the destruction of German cities, and Nazi propaganda stayed too bombastic, too cynical, too short-term and too rigid to be convincing.

When the D-Day landings had succeeded and the advance of the allies was finally under way, the Americans asked the Foreign Office to second Newsome to SHAEF, Eisenhower's Supreme Headquarters Allied Expeditionary Force. So, in September, he joined his staff as head of their Radio Department of Psychological Warfare, based in Paris.

Three months later, he was suddenly transferred to replace the representative of the American Office of War Information in charge of Radio Luxembourg, using their powerful radio transmitter to co-ordinate broadcasts for SHAEF. Radio Luxembourg became another multi-national broadcaster, under Newsome's editorial direction, run jointly by the four belligerent powers plus the Dutch, Czechs and Belgians. Ritchie took over from him in London. Kirkpatrick was also sent to run the British side of the occupation of Nazi Germany.

It was a thrilling time, and Newsome entered Germany with the Seventh Army, and was one of the first to have the horrifying experience, "deeply graven in my memory", of opening the concentration camp at Dachau. He arrived back in Luxembourg just in time to broadcast on the night war ended:

> "And now London and Paris have hailed a great
> and glorious triumph of their nations' arms.
> Together they must take the lead in seeing to it
> that no need will ever arise for a third victory
> won at such heavy cost."

"If I were to try to describe in one word the character which I sought to give our broadcasts I would reply 'civilised'," he said in his farewell talk on Radio Luxembourg on 23 May 1945:

> "There were many who told us that we were
> failing at our task because we did not employ
> tricks and devices as clever as those of the Nazis.

Others said we did not adapt ourselves sufficiently to the tastes and susceptibilities of our audiences. Our bitterest critics were those who objected to admissions that the Allies were far from perfect and had made mistakes, and that our enemies were not all, to a man, woman and child of them, villains beyond redemption. Yet we sought to tell the truth: not only the true facts about the war, but the truth about human beings at all times – that no-one of any race or nation has a monopoly of virtue or viciousness, that in everybody there is a glorious goodness and bestial evil which fight for domination."

It had been deeply controversial, and those arguments are largely forgotten, but they have their echoes today and remain as important as ever. "There were giants in Bush House at that time, and battles of giants," wrote another member of the European Staff, Maurice Latey, later Eastern Europe editor. "At the centre the massive figure of Noel Newsome ... engaged in epic contests with Hugh Greene, in charge of German broadcasts – six or seven feet of quiet implacable determination beside a basilisk stare – and the late Darsie Gillie, in charge of French broadcasts, six or seven feet of gesticulating vehemence which earned him the nick-name of 'the semaphore'."

And the wounds lasted. "Looking back now, when tempers have cooled, I think he was right," wrote one PWE official a generation later, explaining how Newsome ignored their propaganda directives. "But at the time I did not. I was just as critical of him as most of his colleagues were."

During the war, Newsome had survived the active scepticism of Greene. Greene, brother of the novelist Graham Greene, called him "blissfully ignorant of Europe" (contemporary descriptions of Greene were also extreme: "A beast," one of his colleagues said). Newsome even survived one sweaty evening during the North Africa landings, when, according to Brice-Lockhart, he told the minister (Bracken) to 'fuck off', before slamming down the phone.

Bracken forgave him and wrote later to thank him for "the splendid manner in which you have performed one of the really difficult tasks of the war". But this kind of support was not enough to help him survive the peace.

The first shock came from Kirkpatrick. He had put a plan forward to Kirkpatrick before leaving for SHAEF of a joint Allied administration in Berlin, including a joint broadcasting service for Germany and for Europe as a whole, with himself as Director of European Broadcasts. But there was to be no joint Allied administration of Germany.

Newsome then went to see the new BBC director-general William Haley to see if there would be a job for him in the BBC after the war. He said later that Haley told him there would be no important BBC European Service after the war and that he was anyway too much of a crusader to stay with the peacetime BBC. "You have an axe to grind," said Haley. "I'm afraid that if you stayed with the BBC you would give us a headache and break your own heart."

When war finally ended and after his experiences in Europe, Newsome still hoped that the Western Allies would preserve the radio co-operation which they had established. He planned that this would be in Luxembourg and that he could direct it. His idea was to form the basis of an international radio station, dedicated to impartial news and under the control of the United Nations. It was part of his dream of a united Europe, forged by the experience of broadcasting alongside all the nations of western Europe, which had been the basis of the magazine he launched in 1944 called simply *Europe*. The Americans were committed to the idea and so were most of the other European allies. But one of the last decisions of the wartime coalition government had ended British participation in the broadcasting experiment, and abandoned what had become a huge audience across Europe.

It ended Newsome's vision of "an international broadcasting service … for a New Order, in which the nations would cooperate in pooling their new technical skills and their ancient wisdoms to set free mankind from physical misery and despair of the spirit."

Newsome resigned from the BBC to stand as Liberal candidate for Penrith and Cockermouth in the 1945 election, where the vision of a united Europe was one of the planks in his platform. He worked for the Ministry of Coal and Power and as first Director of Public Relations for the new National Coal Board. He was later PR director of tractor pioneer Harry Ferguson Ltd and first director of the Agricultural Training School at Stoneleigh Abbey.

He still had one lasting campaign before him, as the first chairman of the Warwickshire branch of the Conservation Society. In 1973, he was chosen as Midlands Man of the Year for his report on the dumping of cyanide in the Midlands, which led to new legislation to outlaw the indiscriminate dumping of toxic waste, the Deposit of Poisonous Waste Act 1972. He died in 1976, after campaigning for the European side in the referendum the previous year, aged only 69.

Ritchie stayed with the BBC. He was keen to fulfil the promise he had repeated as Colonel Britton and to give the occupied people of Europe their final instructions. And in one last Colonel Britton broadcast from Radio Luxembourg in May 1945, he did so, this time billed as 'The Number One voice from SHAEF'.

"Here is the special order of the day from General Eisenhower, the supreme commander, to the resistance forces of France, Belgium, Holland, Denmark and Norway," he began, going on to congratulate them on their huge sacrifice and to give them their last orders "in this great hour".

In July 1945, there were photos of Ritchie and his wife Evelyn and two children in the national press, after the secret of the identity of Colonel Britton was finally revealed. After the war, he was seconded to British Information Services in New York, as director of their Press and Radio Division. Then it was back to the BBC as General Overseas Services Organiser, and eventually BBC Head of

Publicity from 1950-56. But after recovering from a stroke in 1955, at the age of only 50, he found himself jobless and living with his family in the spare bedrooms of friends.

He retired eventually to Mickleham in Surrey, writing his music, and later wrote about his illness movingly and optimistically in a book called *Stroke*. He died in 1967 aged only 62.

It is worth asking why the legacy, both of the V campaign and of the European Service, has been so little recognised. Both Ritchie and Newsome were awarded medals by other European nations, but not their own (though Newsome was given the OBE).

Something about the European Service still bothers the BBC. Their two-hour epic to celebrate 50 years from VE Day in 1995, a two-part documentary called *What Did You Do in the War Auntie*, devoted just seven minutes to the European Service. Their own official history of the World Service, which both men did so much to shape, mentions Newsome in a small footnote. Only a few of the Colonel Britton broadcasts, or Newsome's *The Man in the Street,* remain in the BBC's archives. The trouble is that, in this case, history was in the hands of Newsome's rivals. Hugh Greene was to inherit the world as director-general.

The reputation of the BBC abroad was largely created by the European Service in wartime, even though it did so outside BBC control. When Mikhail Gorbachev was under house arrest in his dacha after the attempted coup, he said he followed events as they unfolded by listening to the World Service. But the BBC hierarchy never forgave Newsome for his part in the decision to wrest the European Service from their clutches in 1941. He had to wait for the historian Asa Briggs, in his mammoth history of broadcasting in the UK in 1970, to give Newsome his due as "the central figure in the organisation ... and the most industrious, lively and imaginative of all its wartime recruits".

Partly because of this tension, the impact and legacy of the V campaign has not been properly assessed. There were celebrations around VE Day. As late as 1972, Diana Mosley referred to Beethoven's Fifth as the 'V Symphony' in a letter to her sister Nancy Mitford. There were celebrations on the twentieth anniversary in 1961, and at the time Maurice Simon from the Belgian Resistance bore witness to what it meant:

"At the time, I was incarcerated in one of the

occupiers' prisons. I can bear witness to the signal of encouragement which passed between the prisoners by means of knocking out the Morse Vs on the walls of their cells."

There are clues about its legacy, and its relative obscurity, in Ritchie's memo of May 1942, after the V campaign had been brought to a sudden halt. He said that people across Europe were not listening to the BBC primarily for entertainment or self-interest or for complex political reasons. They were listening because they were desperate for the truth and they wanted to hear the British point of view. The failure to provide that, he said, would be to miss a golden opportunity for Britain to speak to the people of Europe as a whole.

And there lies the difficulty, then and now. British policy has always been confused about the UK's relationship with Europe – either ignoring it completely or over-complicating the relationship with excruciating spin, designed to divide nations and interests from each other. Thanks to the European Service, the UK government found itself in 1945 with an extraordinary moral and cultural leadership in Europe, and they flung it away. They could never decide what to say or how to use it.

If this is so, then it follows that the European

Service, and the V campaign, played a central role in the emergence of a European identity. For eleven months, Colonel Britton had spoken over the heads of the factions and nationalities of Europe to its beleaguered people as a whole. He did not create the resistance movements, but he provided a fertile ground for them when there seemed little hope. He did not give birth to them, but the European Service was in a sense their midwife – and, in the rest of their enormous broadcast output in the war years, the midwife of the new post-war Europe. The legacy of both men, Ritchie and Newsome, is a sense of enduring European identity.

It seems strange now, looking back, that there was a time when the BBC – or an organisation paid for by the BBC – spoke to the people of Europe in this way. It seems even stranger that it gave them instructions in subversion and incited them to sabotage. There were parts of the establishment which never forgave this, and parts of the BBC too, but the legacy remains with us.

But, in their confused relationship with continental Europe, the British have forgotten the story.

Short bibliography

Argemi, Marc (2011), 'Government, official rumours and journalism during World War II', Paper to ECREA@LSE, international symposium on 'The Mediation of Scandal and Moral Outrage', 16-18 Dec.

Army Talks (1945), 'Colonel Britton and the V-for-Victory Campaign', Vol. IV, No. 18, 16 Sept.

Balfour, Michael (1979), *Propaganda in War, 1939-1945: Organizations, Policies and Publics in Britain and Germany.* Boston: Routledge & Kegan Paul.

Bergmaier, Horst and Lotz, Rainer E., (1997), *Hitler's Airwaves: The inside story of Nazi radio broadcasting and propaganda swing*, New Haven, Yale University Press.

Asa Briggs (1970), *The History of Broadcasting in the United Kingdom, Vol III: The War of Words,* London: Oxford University Press.

Garnett, David (2002), *The Secret History of the Political Warfare Executive*, London: St Ermin's Press.

Lean, Tangye (1943), *Voices in the Darkness*, London: Secker and Warburg.

Liebling, A. J. (1941), 'Colonel Britton and the rhythm', *New Yorker*, 4 Oct.

Stefanidis, Ioannis (2012), *Substitute for Power: Wartime British Propaganda to the Balkans, 1939–44*, Farnham: Ashgate.

Stenton, Michael (2000), *Radio London and Resistance in Occupied Europe: British political warfare 1939-1943*, Oxford: OUP.

White, John Baker (1955), *The Big Lie*, London: Evans Brothers.

Acknowledgements

I would like to thank the Newsome family for first introducing me to this story, and especially my cousin Penelope Newsome to whom I owe a great deal, not least for helping me by twice reading through this book. Also Adam Ritchie for reading this manuscript and for his help and advice, and to the Newsome and Ritchie families for permission to quote from the unpublished memoirs of the two central characters in this book. I am also particularly grateful to the staff at the London Library and at the Newsome-Ritchie Archive at Churchill College, Cambridge. And to Michael Stenton for his advice. All the mistakes are very definitely mine.

David Boyle
February 2016
South Downs

From Scandal: How homosexuality became a crime

Also by David Boyle and published by The Real Press, available in print and as an ebook (see www.therealpress.co.uk).

It was Saturday 6 April 1895. The weather was windy and drizzly as the passengers packed onto the quayside at Dover to catch the steam packet to Calais, due on the evening tide. Perhaps it was packed that night because of Easter the following week. Perhaps it wasn't as packed as some of the witnesses claimed later, or the downright gossips who weren't actually there. But it was still full. Those waiting on the quay wrapped up warm against the chilly Channel breeze and eyed each other nervously, afraid to meet anyone they knew, desperately wanting to remain anonymous.

Among those heading for France that night was

an American, Henry Harland, the editor and co-founder of the notorious quarterly known as *The Yellow Book*, the journal of avant garde art and writing which had taken England by the scruff of the neck in the 1890s. Harland had come to Europe with his wife Aline, pretending to have been born in St Petersburg and planning to live in Paris, but had instead made his London flat, at 144 Cromwell Road, the very hive of excitement in the literary world. Henry James, Edmund Gosse and Aubrey Beardsley came and went. The parties were talked about with awe and excitement. Henry and Aline always spent the spring in Paris, so they were not leaving the country suddenly and in desperation, but it dawned on them that the reason the quayside was so packed that night was because many others were.

The name of the ferry the Harlands boarded has been lost to history. It was probably the *Victoria* – her sister ship the *Empress* had been badly damaged in a collision the month before and was now in dry dock. There she heaved beside the sea wall, as the muffled passengers filed up the gangway, her twin rakish masts and her twin funnels belching smoke, her two paddlewheels poised to drive across the world's busiest sea lane at 18 knots, her stern flag flapping in the wind with the insignia of the London, Chatham and Dover Railway.

Harland had a good idea why the ferries were full, though he was still surprised. He was also aware of at least some of the implications for himself. Oscar Wilde had been arrested for 'gross indecency' that evening, having lost his libel action the day before. The news of the warrant for his arrest was in the evening papers, and included the information that Wilde had been arrested while he had been reading a copy of *The Yellow Book* (this was quite wrong, in fact; he was reading *Aphrodite* by Pierre Louys). Harland could only guess the motivations of those who were now suddenly crowding across the English Channel, but it looked remarkably like fear. They huddled in corners in the stateroom downstairs, out of the wind, damp and smuts, wondering perhaps whether they would ever see their native land again.

There was an unnerving atmosphere of menace that evening. One item in the evening papers implied that the nation was perched on the edge of a scandal that would make the establishment teeter. "If the rumours which are abroad tonight are proved to be correct we shall have such an exposure as has been unheard of in this country for many years past."

Did it mean the exposure would reach those who run the nation, or did it mean something even more terrifying – that the exposure would spread downwards through society? As the passengers knew only too well, the combination of events which they had feared for a decade had now come to pass. It had been a few months short of ten years since the so-called 'Labouchère amendment' had been rushed through the House of Commons, criminalising homosexual activity of any kind between men. It was never quite clear why women were excluded – there is no evidence for the old story that Queen Victoria claimed it was impossible. For ten years now, they had watched the rising sense of outrage at the very idea of 'homosexuality' – though the term was not yet in common use – and had realised that there might come a time when that law was enforced with an unsurpassed ferocity.

It wasn't that they necessarily had anything to be ashamed of – quite the reverse – but they had reputations to be lived down, some event in their past or some 'unfortunate' relationship behind them. Now that public concern had turned

to what looked like public hysteria, they clearly had to be vigilant. They did not want to be accused, as Oscar Wilde was accused, by a violent aristocrat of doubtful sanity, and would then have to respond in the courts or the press. They could not face the fatal knock on the front door from a smiling acquaintance who would turn out to be a dangerous blackmailer.

But now the unthinkable had happened. Wilde had been stupid enough to sue the Marquess of Queensberry for libel, and had lost. The public had driven each other into a crescendo of rage and it seemed only sensible to lie low in Paris for a while. Or Nice or Dieppe, or the place where the British tended to go in flight from the law – Madrid. Anywhere they could be beyond the reach of the British legal system.

As we shall see, one of those who fled, as I discovered during the research that led to this book, was my own great-great-grandfather – escaping for the second time in a just over a decade, in a story that my own family had suppressed for three generations.

It is no small matter to flee your home and go abroad, especially to do so within the space of a few hours to gather your belongings and make arrangements for your property or your money. As it is, escape was only a solution available to those wealthy enough to flee. It is even tougher perhaps for those in some kind of unconventional relationship, ambiguousto the outside world – but perhaps not ambiguous enough – aware that the decision to go was probably irreversible. It might look like an admission of guilt.

On the other hand, what might happen when the newspapers could unleash this kind of bile? What would happen when they had successfully gaoled Wilde with hard labour and turned on his friends, and anyone else who looked unusual? What would happen if the rumours were correct and the scandal would shortly engulf the government and royal family? Harland did not know at this stage that, when the news about *The Yellow Book* became clear on Monday morning, a mob would gather outside the offices of his publishers Bodley Head, and would break all the windows. "It killed *The Yellow Book* and it nearly killed me," said publisher John Lane later.

We know now that, in the event, the threatened conflagration did not take place, but in the remaining 72 years while Section 11 of the Criminal Law Amendment Act, the Labouchère Amendment, stayed on the statute books, 75,000 were prosecuted under its terms, among them John Gielgud, Lord Montagu and Alan Turing.

Many thousands of lives were ruined – Turing committed suicide not long afterwards, having been forced to undergo hormone treatment that made him grow breasts.

Yet that moment of fear in Britain in 1895, unprecedented in modern times, has been largely forgotten. It is remembered as a sniggering remnant of gossip, about the number of English aristocrats or others in public life, living incognito in Dieppe, or glimpsed in the bars in Paris, and the awareness as a result that they had something to hide. One of the purposes of this book is to remember it for what it was – one of the most disturbing chapters in modern English history, when public horror at sexual behaviour reached such intensity that nobody seemed completely safe, and nobody could be relied on to protect you. And when a man like Wilde, the darling of the theatre critics, with two sell-out shows in London's West End theatres, could be brought low by a furious, litigious pugilist – well, really, who was safe?

This unique moment of fear in English history came at a peculiar moment, at perhaps the apogee of tolerance in so many other ways – women were cycling and getting university degrees, training to be doctors. Mohandas Gandhi was a London-trained barrister working in South Africa. George Bernard Shaw was overturning assumptions about the right way to dress, eat and spell. H. G. Wells was sleeping his way through the ranks of the young female Fabians. Edward Carpenter, in his sandals, was advertising freedom from the constraints of conventional sexuality, having forged a gay relationship with a working class man from Sheffield. William Morris was still, just, preaching a revolution based on medieval arts and crafts. And yet the rage at the idea that men should love each other sexually threatened to overwhelm everything.

That morning, Queensberry had received a telegram from an anonymous supporter, which read: "Every man in the City is with you. Kill the bugger."

Why did it happen? Partly because of growing public concern following the Labouchère amendment, sneaked though Parliament in 1885, but even that was more than the individual brainchild of a lone radical. Why this shift from tolerance of the changing role of women and emerging new ideas to this threatening public rage? How did homosexuality emerge as a key issue in English public life?

The answer lies in the events that took place in

Dublin a decade before, starting with the political aftermath of the murder of Lord Frederick Cavendish, the son of the Duke of Devonshire and the newly-appointed Chief Secretary to Ireland.

But I had a more personal reason for finding out the answers to some of these questions. My family lived in Dublin in the 1880s. The reason that they don't any more, and that I was born in England not Ireland, was because of those same events there in that decade. Until the last few years, when I began researching this book, I was unaware of them.

All I knew was that my great-great-grandfather, the banker Richard Boyle, had left Dublin suddenly and under a cloud around 1884. His photograph has been torn out of the family photo album, with only his forehead remaining. There are no likenesses of him anywhere that I know about. The letters related to these events in the family, and what followed, have long since been destroyed. I believe I was even there when my grandfather burned the last of them on the bonfire around 1975.

I had always been interested in what might

have happened, but had assumed that the memories were now beyond recovery, just as the fate of my great-great-grandfather was lost in the mists of unfathomable time.

As it turned out, I was wrong. I was working on another incident in Irish history in the British Library, and discovered as I did so that a whole raft of Victorian Irish newspapers had been digitised and were now searchable online. On an impulse, I put in the name 'Richard Boyle' and searched through the references in the Dublin papers. Then, suddenly, my heart began beating a little faster, because there it was – the first clue I found to a personal tragedy, and a national tragedy too: this was the spark that lit the fuse which led to the criminalisation of gay behaviour and the great moment of fear that followed the arrest of Oscar Wilde.

That first clue led to others, which led to others. I will never know the whole story, but what I did discover took me on a historical rollercoaster, and an emotional one, which catapulted me back to the strangely familiar world of the end of the nineteenth century – and a glimpse of that sudden fear in April 1895 that drove many of those affected so suddenly abroad....

Read more by buying Scandal...

Other titles by David Boyle

Building Futures
Funny Money: In search of alternative cash
What is New Economics?
The Sum of our Discontent
The Tyranny of Numbers
The Money Changers
Numbers (with Anita Roddick)
Authenticity: Brands, Fakes, Spin and the Lust for
Real Life
Blondel's Song
Leaves the World to Darkness (fiction)
News from Somewhere (*editor*)
Toward the Setting Sun
The New Economics: A Bigger Picture (with
Andrew Simms)
Money Matters: Putting the eco into economics
The Wizard
The Little Money Book
Why London Needs its own Currency
Eminent Corporations (with Andrew Simms)
Voyages of Discovery
The Human Element
On the Eighth Day, God Created Allotments
The Age to Come
What if money grew on trees (*editor*)

Unheard, Unseen: Submarine E14 and the
Dardanelles
Broke: How to survive the middle class crisis
Alan Turing: Unlocking the Enigma
Peace on Earth: The Christmas truce of 1914
Jerusalem: England's National Anthem
Give and Take (with Sarah Bird)
People Powered Prosperity (with Tony Greenham)
Rupert Brooke: England's Last Patriot
How to be English
Operation Primrose
Before Enigma
The Piper (fiction)
Scandal
How to become a freelancewriter

See also our website at www.therealpress.couk